J. Hampton-Moore

A Dozen Roads to Business Success in America

J. Hampton-Moore

A Dozen Roads to Business Success in America

ISBN/EAN: 9783743373198

Manufactured in Europe, USA, Canada, Australia, Japa

Cover: Foto ©ninafisch / pixelio.de

Manufactured and distributed by brebook publishing software (www.brebook.com)

J. Hampton-Moore

A Dozen Roads to Business Success in America

A DOZEN ROADS TO SUCCESS

BEING

GRAPHIC SKETCHES OF TWELVE OF THE MOST
PROMINENT BUSINESS MEN OF
AMERICA

AND SHOWING

HOW THEY BECAME MILLIONAIRES

DESIGNED

TO INSPIRE THE YOUTH OF THIS COUNTRY WITH
A LAUDABLE AMBITION TO ACHIEVE
A LIKE HONORABLE
SUCCESS

---

*ILLUSTRATED WITH A LIFE-LIKE PORTRAIT
OF THE SUBJECT OF EACH
SKETCH*

PHILADELPHIA, PA.
THE GIRARD PUBLISHING COMPANY
1894

COPYRIGHT, 1894.
THE GIRARD PUBLISHING COMPANY.

ALL RIGHTS RESERVED.

PRESS OF
EDWARD STERN & CO.
PHILADELPHIA

CONTENTS.

George W. Childs, by *J. Hampton Moore*, .	7
Stephen Girard, by *J. H. Bechtel*, ...	19
John D. Rockefeller, by *John Wilson*, . . .	33
Philip D. Armour, by *Charles M. Faye*, . .	47
Enoch Pratt, by *Roberdeau Annan McCormick*, ...	61
Leland Stanford, by *George Patrick Brady*,	75
Marshall Field, by *Charles M. Faye*, ...	91
Johns Hopkins, by *Will J. Guard*, ...	105
Claus Spreckels, by *George Patrick Brady*, .	119
George M. Pullman, by *Charles M. Faye*, .	137
Peter Cooper, by *Clifton R. Bechtel*, ...	153
Charles Lewis Tiffany, by *J. H. Bechtel*, . .	173

GEORGE W. CHILDS

IN the galaxy of noted men of the age there is none more universally esteemed for his straightforward business career and general benevolence than George W. Childs, of Philadelphia. It has been the province of this good man to have started poor, with "the odds against him," as the uncouth observer would remark, and to have surmounted the obstacles that came in his way, until he reached the very pinnacle of success. From the lowest rung of the ladder, starting out in Baltimore when twelve years of age, as an errand boy in a book-store, and making $2.00 a week, he persevered until he reached the top—until fame and fortune were his, and all the world felt the better for his being in it. The life of Mr.

Childs has been a forcible example of what an intelligent American boy can accomplish if he sets about his work with an honest purpose and maintains the right course in his dealings with other men. From his earliest boyhood his whole idea of life seems to have been to succeed, to do good, to make friends. In these three particulars he hewed close to the line, with the result of accomplishing all that he set out to do and of achieving a distinction for good sense, philanthropy and popularity seldom enjoyed by mortal man.

Mr. Childs was born in Baltimore, May 12, 1829, and as soon as he was able he sought employment. After one year of running errands for a book-store he entered the United States Navy, and spent fifteen months in the service at Norfolk, after which he went to school at Baltimore to get some educational advantages with which the better to engage in the struggle for a higher position in life. Coming to Philadelphia while yet about fifteen years of age, he secured a place as errand boy and clerk in a book-store at $3.00 per week. This was really the beginning of his business training. He did whatever was required of him, from washing the sidewalk to sweeping the store, but he did it from the conviction, which came to him early, that to succeed in any line one must not overlook the little things nor over-estimate his own importance. His rule was a good one, for his employers observed his diligence and it was not long before the young clerk was sent to New York, Boston and other cities as a buyer for the house. Thus came the reward, and with it the opportunity to enter a larger field. In four years, the young book-buyer, who had popularized himself with the trade, counted up his savings and found that he had enough capital to open a place of his own. He secured a store in the old *Ledger* building and forged ahead in a small way until he became of age. Then he took a partner and went into the book-publishing business. Amongst other books issued by him was "Dr. Kane's Arctic Explorations," which found an immense sale and brought in a great deal of money. The business continued to prosper, and after a few years enabled the energetic young publisher to embark upon the greatest and proudest business enterprise of his life.

When he opened his little store in the old *Ledger* Building, the lad, for he was still in his teens, formed in his mind a determination to some day become the owner of the *Ledger* itself. This was the enterprise upon which he staked all the earnings that had come to him through his store and publishing business. It was in 1864, when the owners of the paper were losing enormous sums of money, and were wrangling over the war policy to be pursued, that Mr. Childs offered to buy them out. They sold to him for upwards of $150,000, and people wondered if he had not made a poor bargain. That remained to be seen. The new owner had new ideas, but he had more than that. He had a conviction that a paper could be made influential and profitable if it published the news truly, avoided sensationalism and suggestiveness, and adhered to honest principles and high moral ideas. That his views were correct ones, the future amply demonstrated, for in spite of his raising the price of advertisements, and of the paper itself from one to two cents, confidence was restored, the circulation was increased, and the income was correspondingly augmented. In three years (1867) the new *Public Ledger* Building was erected at an enormous outlay and was pronounced by the many eminent men who attended the dedicatory ceremonies to be the finest newspaper building in the world. In that great building, at Sixth and Chestnut Streets, Mr. Childs now employs about 500 people who, without exception, look up to him with unfeigned respect as a generous, magnanimous and exceptional employer. For upwards of twenty-five years, Mr. Childs has had his office in this building, where he has not only given personal attention to business matters, but has mapped out schemes of philanthropy until thousands of people, some of them in foreign climes, sing his praises for the good that he has done. Here also he has entertained distinguished men and women of all countries, who, knowing of his benevolence and public spirit, have esteemed it an honor to meet him. Nor have the great people of the earth been his only visitors. In all his prosperity, in the midst of all his business, never a day passes that the poor have not also been admitted and remembered. It is one of the kindliest characteristics of this amiable man that he recognizes "a man's a man for a' that." But the man whom George W. Childs likes perhaps best of all his visitors is the man who, like himself, is not ashamed of work, and not too proud to begin at the beginning.

Of Mr. Childs' visitors, columns upon columns of interesting matter could be written. General Grant was his intimate friend. So were Sherman and Sheridan. He was the friend of Dickens, of Longfellow, of Dean Stanley. Dom Pedro and a host of foreign notables have been entertained by him. In fact, so great is his fame abroad that distinguished men travelling to this country anticipate with pleasure a meeting with him and a share in his hospitality. Philadelphia has no greater entertainer than he. He stands at the head of all the citizens of the State as the host and friend of eminent strangers.

These associations with foreigners have resulted in the performance by Mr. Childs of many acts of philanthropy abroad, of which little is known. Some of his acts, however, may be judged from his erection of a magnificent drinking fountain in honor of Shakespeare at Stratford-on-Avon, and in providing costly memorial windows in Westminster Abbey to Cowper and other English poets.

The vast amount of good that Mr. Childs has been pleased to do for his own countrymen and countrywomen it would take much more time than can be given here to tell about. To newspaper men and ministers of the Gospel who needed a helping hand he has been a generous friend; to young people, and especially the daughters or orphans of literary men and worthy acquaintances, he has been a kind adviser and benefactor. From 300 to 400 girls, coming under this classification, have been educated by him, some of them, having special aptitudes, having been sent to Paris, Berlin, Vienna and elsewhere in this and other countries to complete their educations. The proper training of young people has always been a favorite topic with him, and his counsels on this subject entered largely into the construction by his lamented friend, Anthony J. Drexel, of the great Drexel Institute in Philadelphia. Although the expense of fitting out this magnificent and costly institution was borne solely by Mr. Drexel, Mr. Childs watched every move concerning it, and while he lives will probably be its chief guardian. Affections of thirty years bound these two men, Drexel and Childs, together like brothers, and what one undertook the other usually endorsed. It had been so in a thousand projects, undertakings and charities, but it was conspicuously so in the case of the Drexel Institute.

There was one other instance which should be mentioned here—the presentation by Childs and Drexel to the International Typographical Union, in 1886, of a check for $10,000, with which to start a fund for a home for union printers. Mr. Childs had always been an avowed friend of the workingman. He has shown his interest in many ways. He provided a beautiful burial-ground for printers in Woodlands Cemetery. When the union rate for setting type was reduced by the union from forty-five to forty cents a thousand ems he declined to avail himself of the reduction. He was getting as much as ever for advertisements, he said, and he would continue to pay the old rate of wages, though it cost him $12,000 a year.

When Mr. Drexel joined him in presenting the check to the printers, labor was restive and capital uneasy. No better test of his friendship for labor was needed. The gift was an inspiration to the printers and they began at once to swell the fund. In a few years they erected, at Colorado Springs, a $60,000 home, which they called the "Childs-Drexel Home for Union Printers." They paid for it, and to-day dozens of aged and infirm men are enjoying within its walls or about its beautiful grounds all the comfort that can be vouchsafed them in the closing years of their lives.

What the outside world thinks of Mr. Childs his own employés think of him. None begrudge him his prosperity or his wealth, and all wish him an increase of the blessings of life. In these days of bickerings and jealousy in the world of labor and capital, what higher compliment can be paid an employer than this! His men love him. Say what you may about chiefs of staff or about each other, but say nought against George W. Childs! His every impulse is kindly. Men tire from the steady pursuit of duty, and he grants them a respite with a financial Godspeed. They wait the coming of the festive Christmas season with misgivings, and he gladdens their hearts with substantial tokens of his appreciation. He forgets not the halt and infirm in his employ. When good men die he comforts their families. Ask a *Ledger* man his opinion of George W. Childs, and there is but one answer. It is an answer full of admiration, of gratitude, of respect.

STEPHEN GIRARD

STEPHEN GIRARD

THE subject of this sketch, whose portrait we herewith present to our readers, was one of Philadelphia's wealthiest and most successful merchants, and one of the first to devote his wealth to the establishment of an educational institution.

He was born near Bordeaux, France, on the 20th of May, 1750. His father and his grandfather were both sea captains, and men of considerable influence. Stephen evidently inherited from his ancestors his strong love for the sea, and because his wishes to become a sailor were opposed by his father, and also because of his dislike to his step-mother, he left home at a very early age to enter upon a maritime career, without having received more than a rudimentary education.

He had two brothers, John and Etienne, who were both well educated. John became a merchant and ship-owner and Etienne, in the second year of the French Republic, was Secretary-General of the district of Bordeaux.

At the age of twenty-four, Stephen had already risen to the position of master and captain of a ship. His first mercantile venture was to San Domingo, in February, 1774. He traded for several years between New York and the ports of New Orleans and Port au Prince. It was on one of these voyages that, becoming befogged off the Delaware Capes, and being made aware of the risk he would incur if he persisted in going on to New York, for Admiral Howe's ships of war were then skirting the New Jersey coast in search of American cruisers, he was induced to sail up the Delaware to Philadelphia to avoid capture, and, in May, 1777, gave up the sea for a mercantile life. He opened a small shop on Water Street above Market, and, from the outset, was quite successful.

He would occasionally go as master of one

of his ships, leaving the conduct of his store to those in his employ whose faithful service he could well trust. It was on one of these voyages to San Domingo, that his vessel was captured, and he returned a poorer, though perhaps a wiser, man.

In June, 1777, he married Miss Mary Lumm, daughter of a caulker, who is said to have been very pretty. His only child died in infancy.

Girard heartily espoused the cause of the American Revolution and aided it in various ways. He made his home at Mount Holly, New Jersey, while the British occupied Philadelphia.

In 1782, he took a lease on a number of stores on Water Street, which proved to be a very profitable venture. Ritter, in " Philadelphia and her Merchants," says that in 1791, Girard kept a green grocery and provision store at 43 North Front Street, occupying through to and including 31 Water Street. He probably rebuilt or remodelled his Water Street front, for it is known that his residence and his counting-house were under the same roof, with his pier or wharf directly in front. Unlike most merchants of to-day, he preferred to reside amid the scenes of his business activities.

His brother John, who for a time resided in San Domingo, came to Philadelphia and engaged in business with Stephen, but failing to agree, the partnership was dissolved, John retiring with $60,000 and Stephen with $30,000. It was about this time that Stephen engaged in trade with the East Indies, and from this time forward, when he was over forty years of age, his fortune increased very rapidly.

When the charter of the old United States Bank expired in 1810–11, he purchased, through Baring's, London, about $500,000 of that stock. Soon after, he secured title to the banking house, on South Third Street, and in May, 1812, just at the opening of the war with Great Britain, he started his own private bank, with a capital of $1,200,000. This was a bold venture just at the opening of hostilities with a foreign power, but the notes of his bank were always counted as good as gold.

When the new United States Bank was organized in 1816, he waited until the last moment before the subscription books were closed, then, inquiring if all that wished had subscribed, he coolly took the balance of the stock, amounting to $3,100,000. Trusting implicity in his own judgment, he was fond of making such bold strokes, and of surprising the more cautious and timid of his friends. His own bank at the time of his death, which occurred on December 26, 1831, had accumulated about $4,000,000.

During the war of 1812, he rendered valuable service to the Government by placing at its disposal the resources of his bank at a time of difficulty and embarrassment, subscribing to a large loan which the Government had vainly sought to obtain.

He was greatly interested in the welfare of his adopted city. He gave a portion of his time, for several years, to the management of municipal affairs, and rendered efficient service as Warden of the Port and as Director of many public institutions.

While he often seemed cold and uncharitable, yet, under that rough exterior, there dwelt a generous heart. This was probably never more strikingly manifest than during the epidemic of yellow fever, in 1793, and again in 1798, which swept away one-sixth of the population of Philadelphia. When, during its height, a hospital was established, for which it seemed almost impossible to secure competent management, Girard devoted himself personally, fearless of all risks, to the care of the sick and the burial of the dead, not only in the hospital, of which he became manager, but throughout the city, supplying the poor sufferers with money and provisions. Two hundred children, made orphans by the ravages of the fever, were, in a great measure, thrown upon his care.

The breadth of his interest is shown in the largeness of the scope of his benefactions. His fortune, which amounted to about $7,500,000, was widely and wisely distributed. To the College which bears his name, and which, at that time, was probably the largest private charity in the world, he gave property then worth about $6,000,000. To the Pennsylvania Hospital he gave $30,000; to the Deaf and Dumb Asylum, $20,000; to the Orphan Asylum, $10,000; to the Lancaster schools, $10,000; to the Society for the Relief of Distressed Sea Captains, $10,000; to the Masonic Grand Lodge, $20,000; to the Corporation of Philadelphia for City Improvements, $500,000; to the State of Pennsylvania for her canals, $300,000; for the purpose of providing fuel for the poor of Philadelphia, $10,000; for the establishment of a Free School in Passyunk, $6,000; and to the city of New Orleans for municipal improvements, he gave a portion of his valuable estate in Louisiana.

He gave to his surviving brother and eleven of his nieces, sums ranging from $5,000 to $20,000; to one niece, who was the mother of a large family, he gave $60,000. Nor was he forgetful of his employés. To each of the captains in his service at his death, he gave $1,500; to each of his apprentices, $500; and to his old servants he gave life annuities, ranging from $300 to $500 each, to be paid in quarterly instalments.

While Girard was very plain in his style of dress, and indifferent to the changes of fashion, yet in his dress and surroundings he was scrupulously neat and clean, and the materials of his clothing were of the very best quality. His house on Water Street was furnished in the costliest style. The floors, mantels, and table tops were of Italian marble. Turkey and brussels carpets covered his floors, and his drawing-room furniture was made in Paris.

He was very fond of animals, and his horses, dogs and pigeons were of the finest breeds. He was also fond of gardening, and his fruits and vegetables received much of his personal care.

In his earlier life, it is said, his table was noted for the abundance and perfection of its supplies, not only from his own gardens and farms, but also from foreign countries. He became more abstemious, however, in later life.

Girard was regarded by many as being cold and unsympathetic, yet he had, throughout his long life, many fast friends. He was, at times, quite irritable, and would often break out upon his dependents in his broken English with great volubility.

His chief delight was in seeing his wealth usefully employed. He built many houses which were always neat and substantial in their construction, but without ornamentation. He also built many ships which were a source of large profit to him. He is said to have been the first person to lengthen a ship by cutting her through the middle and inserting a piece, one of his own vessels having been so lengthened according to his own plans.

He was very fond of children, and not only educated many, but looked after their welfare after their education was finished. The sums he gave to eleemosynary objects during his lifetime were usually small, and few persons dared approach him to solicit aid for charitable purposes.

It is related that, upon one occasion, Samuel Coates, a shrewd Quaker, called to solicit a contribution to the Pennsylvania Hospital. "Call to-morrow," said Girard, "and if you find me in the right humor, I may give you something." He called early next morning. "Well," said Girard, "what have you come for, Samuel?" "Anything thee pleases, Stephen." Girard gave him a check for $200, which Samuel put into his pocket. "What! don't you look at the check I give?" "No, Stephen; beggars must not be choosers." "Hand me back that check again," demanded Girard. "No, no, Stephen; 'a bird in the hand is worth two in the bush.'" "By George!" exclaimed Girard, "you have caught me on the right footing this time." He then drew a check for $500, and, presenting it to Mr. Coates, asked him to look at it. "Well, to please thee, Stephen, I will." "Now give me back the first check," demanded Girard, which was instantly complied with.

Upon another occasion, a gentleman with less tact came soliciting aid for some worthy cause, and upon looking at the check which was handed to him, mildly intimated that Girard's means led the recipient to expect a larger amount, whereupon Girard took the check, and after destroying it, dismissed the gentleman without a penny.

His eccentricity and shrewdness are also shown in the following incident: Girard had a cargo of salt lying at his wharf, which one of his principal customers was anxious to secure, but tried to beat down the price. After a time Girard, becoming impatient, cried out to his porter: "Tom, why don't you buy that cargo?" Tom laughingly replied: "Why, sir; I have no money. How can I buy it?" "Never mind that," said Girard. "You take it, and sell it by the load, and pay me as you sell it." Tom took the hint. His customer was foiled, and Tom flourished many years after as a successful salt merchant.

JOHN D. ROCKEFELLER

JOHN D. ROCKEFELLER.

MR. JOHN D. ROCKEFELLER, of the Standard Oil Company, is said to be the richest man in the United States, and he probably is. His fortune has recently been estimated at $125,000,000, and it is probably considerably more. This is a greater amount of wealth than is possessed by any individual member of the European family of the Rothschilds, their fortunes being supposed to average $75,000,000 each. No man living has made money so fast as Mr. Rockefeller. All these millions have been accumulated since 1864. Let us see how he did it.

The Rockefeller family settled in Moravia, N. Y., and subsequently at Owego, in the same State. The father of John D., who was of Scotch extraction, practised medicine, but not very perseveringly, and it is alleged led a somewhat shiftless life. The old farm-house at Owego, in which the family lived, is still standing and was then, and is now, owned by Mr. C. M. LaMonte. The Rockefeller boys did considerable work for farmers in the neighborhood of Owego. Mr. LaMonte says that the first twenty-five cents John Rockefeller ever earned was for work on LaMonte's farm. The boys were not, however, obliged to work in order to get food, but, like most country boys, preferred to earn pocket-money of their own. John had the reputation among the farmers of being a trifle lazy, but even at this age he showed signs of the strong will, calm judgment and perseverance which have become marked characteristics with him in later life. The boys attended school at the Owego Academy, of which Mr. Smyth, now editor of the *Owego Times*, was principal.

Mrs. Rockefeller, the mother of the boys, was a woman of strong character, and was generally admired by her neighbors. She was a strict disciplinarian in her family. It is said that at one time, when she was ill in bed, she compelled John to cut a willow switch, bring it to her, stand by the bed, and take a flogging for some boyish misconduct. She brought her children up religiously and well, and, although strict with them, retained their respect and affection as long as she lived. Benjamin West said that a kiss from his mother made him a painter, and it is not unlikely that the strictness of their mother helped, considerably, to make the Rockefeller boys successful men. The family remained at Owego five or six years, and in 1853 removed to Cleveland, O.

At the time of this removal, John D. was about fourteen years of age. For three years he went to school. When he was nineteen he became a bookkeeper for a produce commission firm in Cleveland, and subsequently was admitted a partner. This partnership continued until 1865. Three years before, however, he, with Clark, his partner, and one or two others, had built a little petroleum refinery up the river. In this enterprise Rockefeller and Clark had put about $4,000. Clark bought Rockefeller's interest in the commission house, and Rockefeller and Samuel Andrews became sole owners of the refinery. When Rockefeller was a bookkeeper, Andrews was a porter in another produce store, down the street. They became acquainted, and as Andrews had accumulated a few hundred dollars and was a practical man, Rockefeller invited him to become a partner in the refinery. At this time Rockefeller was twenty-six years old, and Andrews a year or two younger. The latter had considerable practical ability, and had discovered a way of refining by which more kerosene could be got out of a barrel of petroleum than by any other method. The young refiners very soon met the fate common to nearly all men of enterprise, that of being crippled from lack of adequate capital, for John D. had induced his brother William to establish another refinery. Finally, both refineries were consolidated and a warehouse for the sale of the product was opened in New York. There was no doubt of the prosperity of their business, but they were threatened with ruin before they could get returns from their investment. John D. started out, in Cleveland, to see if he could not get some financial relief. He found S. V. Harkness, a rich whiskey distiller, whose son-in-law, Henry M. Flagler, was not prospering in the salt and lumber business, near Saginaw, Mich. Harkness advanced $60,000 to Rockefeller, and called his son-in-law in from the pine woods, and the new firm of Rockefeller, Andrews & Flagler was started. Flagler's connection with the firm, apart from the pecuniary aid, resulted very advantageously, for he developed remarkable talents in the manipulation of the market for petroleum. In dealing with opposing refiners he went as far as the law would permit. He argued that there was neither feeling nor friendship in trade, consequently, when he got his business enemy in a hole, he squeezed him.

In 1870, the Standard Oil Company was formed, with a capital stock of $1,000,000, with John D. Rockefeller as its President.

He originated the idea of one great concern that should control all the petroleum in the country. Refineries in New York and oil lands in Pennsylvania were purchased. The capital of the corporation was increased to $2,500,000, and a yearly business aggregating $25,000,000 transacted immediately thereafter. Subsequently the capital was increased to $70,000,000, and a handsome dividend was declared yearly thereafter.

The Standard remained in absolute control of the oil business until 1880, and its profits ranged from $8,000,000 to $14,000,000 annually. In virtue of its position it commanded unusual favors from the railroads. It owned all the oil cars run over the New York Central and all that road's terminal facilities for oil.

Commodore Vanderbilt used to say that there was but one man who could dictate to him, and that man was Rockefeller. Ultimately the railroads broke away from the Standard and offered every refiner in the country fair play and no favors. The Standard retaliated by building pipe lines and transporting its oil in them rather than by railway, and the end of this fight was that the Standard became so independent that they did not care what the railroads did, and soon brought the latter to terms.

Many legislative committees in various States and of the Federal Government itself have tried again and again to find out the particulars of the agreements of the various combinations and sub-combinations which go together to make up the syndicate known as the Standard Oil Company. Their efforts have been in vain. The New York counsel of the company issued, a short time ago, under pressure of legal proceedings, what was said to be a copy of the agreement, and it was given to the press. It did not throw much light on the plan and scope of this peculiar arrangement.

The benefit to the consumer of oil, by this concentration of capital, has been made very manifest. Mr. David A. Wells, in his invaluable book, entitled "Recent Economic Changes," says "the annual product of crude petroleum in the United States—the chief source of supply—increased from 9,893,786 barrels in 1873, to 28,249,597 in 1887. The price of crude oil during this period declined from 9·42 cents to 1·59 cents per gallon, and of refined oil from 23·59 cents to 6·75 cents per gallon. The decline in the price of crude oil was unquestionably due to its enormous supply, which at one time amounted to nearly 100,000 barrels per day, while the stock of crude oil rose from 3,500,000 barrels in 1876 to the stupendous figures of 41,000,000 in 1884. Had refined oil declined only at the same rate, its minimum price would have been 15·75 cents per gallon. But the fall in refined oil has been 9·01 cents per gallon greater than the fall in crude oil; and as over 1,000,000,000 gallons were consumed in 1887, this saving of 9·01 cents per gallon to the public amounted to nearly $100,000,000 for that same year."

This reduction, Mr. Wells claims, is largely due to the Standard Oil Company "which, commanding millions of capital, has used it most skilfully in promoting consumption, and in devising and adopting a great number of ingenious methods whereby the cost of production has been reduced to an extent that at the outset would not have seemed possible."

Mr. J. D. Rockefeller would be fully entitled to the claim of a benefactor, in the industrial world, if he had not done anything else than reduce the price of illuminating oil to so low a figure as to bring it within the reach of the poorest householder. He has, however, done far more than this; he is identified with the Baptist denomination, has strong religious convictions, and has contributed munificently not only to help forward the work of his own cherished faith, but to every movement having for its object the intellectual and spiritual development of mankind. Mr. Rockefeller, it has been reported, has said that he was stimulated to this princely giving by listening to the testimony of a working-woman, at one of the denominational meetings, telling in her simplicity, how much of her hard-earned income she set aside for charitable and religious purposes. It was a kind of search-light to

Mr. Rockefeller's conscience, and it led to an introspection on his part, that resulted in the inquiry, "If that poor working-woman does that, what ought I to do?" Mr. Rockefeller's great gifts to religious and educational purposes may be dated from that memorable evening.

Mr. Rockefeller's most recent and noble gifts have been to the Chicago University, and their munificence has been so striking that the Trustees adopted a new seal of the Institution a few months ago, upon which are engraved the words "The University of Chicago, founded by John D. Rockefeller." This is intended to be a new educational centre for the West, patterned largely after the universities of Germany. Large option as to studies and period of study will be given to the under-graduate. He may take his vacation when he pleases; he may take as much as he pleases, and the papers he receives will be granted on the sole basis of study and attainment. In this broad scheme of liberal training there will be open to the election of the student the school of philosophy, of political economy, of history, of mathematics, of English, German and French literature, of Greek, of Latin, of Semitic languages, of physics, of biology, of anthropology, of civil engineering, etc.—twenty-two departments in all. Post-graduate and university extension work will receive special attention.

It was in 1886, that Mr. Rockefeller made public announcement that he would give $600,000 towards strengthening the Chicago University, if others would, through the Baptist Educational Society, bring it up to $1,000,000. This sum of $400,000 was secured, chiefly through the liberality of citizens of Chicago. In September, 1890, Mr. Rockefeller gave another $1,000,000; and in February, 1892, another $1,000,000; and his gift to the Institution, Christmas, 1892, was another $1,000,000 in gold bonds. Other millionaires were stimulated by Mr. Rockefeller's generosity.

For example, Mr. Marshall Field gave the University grounds, said to be worth $600,000. Mr. C. T. Yerkes has recently given $500,000 for the telescope and observatory.

Mr. Rockefeller had a genius for getting and a genius for giving. This latter characteristic is made very manifest in his recent benefactions. If we are, as Mr. Lowell has described his own country, "the most common-schooled and the least cultivated people in the world," then these gifts to the Chicago University are in a right direction. The very core of our national life will be corrupted, if our unprecedented material prosperity is not chastened by the substitution, here and there, of idealizing and refining influences. Mr. Rockefeller, apparently, has noticed the tendency and is doing his part to prevent the United States from sharing the fate of all nations, "where wealth accumulates and men decay."

PHILIP D. ARMOUR

PHILIP D. ARMOUR

FROM a stingy, hard-scrabble farm in Northern New York to the foremost place in the business life of the great middle West, is the eventful path Philip D. Armour has been travelling for sixty-one years, and always on the sunny side. His gains in dollars foot up into dizzy millions, and no man cares less for money or what it will buy for himself than Mr. Armour.

He was born in Stockbridge Hills, Madison County, New York, May 16, 1832, of the traditional "poor but honest parents," and during the first twenty years of life he "farmed it" nine months of the year, and went to a country school the remaining three, managing to get a few finishing touches at the Town Academy, in Watertown, N. Y., from which august institution he was expelled because, contrary to the blue laws of the faculty, he took a pretty girl riding. This expulsion sent into the whirl of commercial life one of the biggest and brainiest men of his time, and gave to Chicago a citizen of unsullied reputation, a lover of his home and family and his fellow-creatures, a prodigal giver to the unfortunate, and a man whose genial temperament, splendid health and spirits, and great business ability make him a tonic to his friends.

In the early spring of 1852, Mr. Armour joined a California party at Oneida, N. Y., and reached the diggings six months later, after a perilious overland journey. Four years later, he returned to the old home in Stockbridge Hills, with a lot of experience and a few hard-earned dollars. Three weeks in New York State satisfied him, and he again joined the star of empire, this time stopping at Milwaukee, Wis., where he entered into a partnership with Frederick B. Miles, in the commission business, and stuck to it until 1863, when his firm was dissolved after a prosperous run. Then Mr. Armour entered into business relations with John Plankington, and together they built up the greatest provision and grain enterprise in the world. In 1864, Mr. Armour had a million. Just before the close of the war, in the spring of 1865, pork was selling at $40 a barrel, and New York speculators were eagerly buying futures at that figure, predicting that it would advance to $60 a barrel. Mr. Armour thought differently, and so did Mr. Plankington, and Armour hurried to New York with every available dollar at his back and began the sensational selling of pork at $40 just so far as the excited New Yorkers would buy. Three days later, the market weakened, Richmond fell, Grant and Lee met under the apple-tree, and pork dropped to $18. Armour and Plankington were richer by many millions. Then began the vast branching out of Plankington and Armour, and, later, of Philip D. Armour and his brothers, until to-day the business is planted in many prominent cities East and West. One pointer as to the real extent of the Armour business is the absolute fact that the distributive sales of the Chicago house alone are greater by millions than the gross receipts of any railroad corporation in the world.

"How much are you worth?" the writer asked Mr. Armour.

"You'll have to talk to Mrs. Armour about that."

"No, not that kind of worth; how much in dollars?"

"How much in dollars?" repeated the packer. He thoughtfully brushed imaginary straws from his whiskers, looked comically solemn for a moment and then said: "I don't know—do you?"

The fame of Philip D. Armour as the ruler of the provision market is as wide as the world, and the prevailing opinion is that he has been uniformly successful in his ventures. In 1878, he was compelled to walk open-eyed into a trap set for him by rivals on the Chicago Board of Trade. These brilliant gentlemen thought it about the proper thing to sell Mr. Armour a few millions of barrels of pork which they didn't happen to have on hand. Away went the market, and Mr. Armour, serene and smiling as the fairest day in June, went down into his money-bag and gave the market about $1,500,000 worth of bracing, his rivals chuckling and rubbing their itching palms in great satisfaction. Mr. Armour took all the pork (?) they offered, and then, just to be good-natured, started to buying on the side. The tide changed, the market boomed, the money-bag got back its own, and some dozens of Board of Trade gentlemen paid Mr. Armour about two millions of dollars for their fun. The story of the pork deal has been repeated again and again in the grain market, and millions continue to roll into that money-bag.

Outside of his packing industries, Mr. Armour has a number of large interests. He is practically the owner of the Chicago, Milwaukee and Saint Paul Railway, one of the greatest corporations of this or any other country—a railroad holding a position in the West about equal in value and importance to the Pennsylvania Railroad in the East.

He is a Director in the company, and this is the only office of any sort he has ever held.

The Armour commercial enterprise employs between 16,000 and 17,000 men, boys and women, and of this vast army not one is debarred from calling on Mr. Armour with any grievance he may have, and many of his old and trusted employés address him as "Phil." The main plant is at the Union Stock Yards, Chicago, and the second largest is at Kansas City, Mo., each division having about sixty branches located in its own territory. In the General Office of the Stock Yards plant, 500 clerks are employed, while at the Executive Office on La Salle Street, Chicago, nearly 200 high class men are grouped about their chief, and he knows every one of them by name.

In the line of grain elevators, Mr. Armour heads the greatest combination in the world, which owns six immense structures with storage capacity of 10,000,000 bushels. Added to this, he is heavily interested in Lake transportation, controlling a company owning four big propellers.

Two treasures possessed by Mr. Armour are prized above all his wealth—Jonathan Ogden Armour is one; Philip D. Armour, Jr., is the other, both under thirty, both married to beautiful women, and both built on the happy, hearty, free-handed plan of their father, with the gentle, smiling manner of the mother, who was Malvina Belle Ogden, daughter of Jonathan Ogden, of Cincinnati, when, in October, 1862, she was married to the man who has never ceased to be her lover. The Armour boys are models. They will carry the name of Armour untarnished to success every hour they live.

The home life of Philip D. Armour is of the most lovable character. Within the plain house on Prairie Avenue, Mr. Armour finds the greater part of his enjoyment, away from business. He cares little for clubs, less for grand opera and "functions" of other sorts, and scarcely knows what the inside of a theatre looks like. He is a plain citizen in every sense of the word, and never conceals his impatience over vulgar parade of wealth.

No man is more neat or methodical in his work than Mr. Armour, and no one of the 15,000 people in his employment works so hard or so many hours, day after day. Think of a man with anywhere from $20,000,000 to $50,000,000, seated at breakfast with his wife at 5.30 o'clock every work-day morning! At 6.15 to 6.30 o'clock the plain carriage is at the door of the plain house and bears away to a plain desk a very plain man, who never fails the hour of seven o'clock in the morning to begin the tasks of the day. And, almost every night, nine o'clock finds the great packer in his bed, which has been his programme ever since his removal from Milwaukee to Chicago, in 1875. He is seldom from home at night unless attending an early evening dinner at the Commercial Club or an important meeting of the Armour Mission, which is the pet of his life. When he feels the absolute need of rest and change, he decides in the morning that he will leave in the afternoon, goes to New York, catches a French or English steamer, and breathes freedom in

Europe for a few weeks. No fuss, no preparation, no wasting of nervous energy "getting ready." And this perhaps is the predominating characteristic of the man—quick decision, producing immediate results.

The City Mission, which bears his family name, was founded in November, 1886, owing its origin to $100,000 bequeathed to such an institution in the will of Joseph F. Armour, a brother, who died in 1881. Joseph entrusted to Philip the perfecting of his idea, and wisely so. Philip loved his big-hearted brother, and at once became deeply interested in the work left him. He increased the bequest to $1,000,000, got his two good boys into the enterprise, and then incorporated the Armour Mission Company under the laws of the State. Once more the practical side of Mr. Armour's charities came to the top. In order to provide an unfailing source of revenue for the Mission, he bought ground near-by and erected a splendid system of tenant buildings, containing 211 apartments, which are rented for an average of $27 per month to nearly 1,200 souls, and the aggregate net rental is applied to the support of the Mission. The work of this Mission is to promote the physical, intellectual and moral improvement of children and youth, and stands on the broad, unsectarian platform of practical Christianity. It is free and open to all, regardless of race or creed. Mr. Armour persists in holding to the old-fashioned idea that prevailed in Stockbridge Hills, fifty years ago, that children develop into manhood and womanhood very much as they are trained and surrounded in their earliest days, and that many a good man and woman can be given to the world by a kindly hand extended to the waif of the street. He loves children, which is the best thing the writer, after a business and social acquaintance of more than twenty years, can say of "Phil" Armour.

Armour Mission auditorium will hold 1,300 people, and by throwing open sliding doors the great Sunday-school gatherings of 2,500 children and teachers are accommodated. The week is filled in with Bible meetings, drill classes, and social sessions. A day nursery, a kindergarten, an industrial school and a free medical dispensary are among the features of the Mission, and the comfortable figure and satisfied face of Mr. Armour are often seen at the various meetings.

Mr. Armour's latest charity is the Armour Institute for boys and girls, representing an investment approximating $1,000,000. The work of this institute will be high-grade manual training, and in addition to this, there will be departments of cooking, dressmaking, millinery, etc., for the girls, with a night school of the best pattern as the top feather. This enterprise is under the captaincy of the Rev. Dr. Frank Gunsaulus, the brilliant pastor of Plymouth Congregational Church, where the Armours worship.

Philip D. Armour may be summed up as a model American business man with not a "bad habit" to blot his escutcheon. He kisses his wife and hugs his big sons—rather an extraordinary condition of affairs in the World's Fair year of 1893.

CHARLES M. FAYE.

ENOCH PRATT

ENOCH PRATT

WHILE Mr. Enoch Pratt, of Baltimore, is not such a multi-millionaire as Rockefeller, the oil prince, or as the Vanderbilts or Goulds, the railway kings, yet as a public benefactor, he is none the less entitled to rank as the peer of any.

In him we find a man who deliberately divested himself of more than a million dollars while yet in the prime of his business career, and while possessed of health that warranted the expectation of living many years to handle that vast sum in the accumulation of yet other millions, to carry out a benefaction whose usefulness will continue to expand with the progress of the years and with the increase of the population of the Commonwealth.

Enoch Pratt comes of a family well-known in New England. His parents, Isaac and Naomi (Keith) Pratt, lived in North Middleborough, Mass., where the son, in whose name and reputation they were destined to live, was born to them in the year 1808.

Of moderate circumstances, they appreciated the advantages of education sufficiently to keep young Enoch at the Bridgewater Academy till his graduation, at the age of fifteen years. He is said to have given but little evidence of more than ordinary shrewdness, though he was obstinate, tenacious of purpose and honest in his opinions, and yet gentle withal in voice and manner. That he was restless and anxious to be self-supporting is shown by his writing a relative in Boston some five weeks before his graduation, asking him to look out for a situation for him, as he thought he could "do considerable business."

His wish was soon gratified, as he was shortly introduced into a wholesale house in that city, where he remained till he was twenty-one years of age, and by contact with the shrewd New England traders of the old days doubtless imbibed the doctrines of economy and conservatism that have been the mainspring of his financial success.

As he attained his majority, he became eagerly ambitious to direct business affairs of his own; so looked about for a new field. Baltimore, at the head of tide-water and navigation, was attracting considerable attention and emigration, as the city was then on the high road to the position it held, from the thirties to the sixties, of being almost the foremost city in maritime affairs in the country.

In these early days many New Englanders removed to the Monumental City. Their intermarriage with its sterling daughters has not a little affected the city's history, and many families now look back with pride to their New England ancestry.

Communicating with relatives in Baltimore, he finally decided to make that city his home, and at once established himself as a commission merchant.

His ability and push were soon recognized, and he later founded the wholesale iron house of Pratt & Keith, and subsequently that of Enoch Pratt & Brothers, which firm continues to-day, being conducted by himself and brother-in-law.

In 1837, he was married to Miss Louisa Hyde, a descendant, on her father's side, of the earliest settlers of Massachusetts. Her mother's people located in Baltimore a century and a half ago, and were of German descent. They have had no children. His business prospering, he early began to take an active interest in enterprises intimately connected with the city. These were the infant days of railways and steam navigation, and their future was considered doubtful by most of the foremost men of the country. His foresight recognized the possibilities of these new and powerful aids to progress. He identified himself with railways and boat lines connecting this city with the South.

These lines have been among the most prolific sources of Baltimore's growth. Without their support it could not have maintained its supremacy as the leading jobbing city of the South.

He became prominently identified with the Philadelphia, Wilmington and Baltimore Railroad, and, as Director and Vice-President, has served that corporation for more than thirty years.

He was one of the organizers and for more than half a century has acted as Director and President of the National Farmers' and Planters' Bank of Baltimore.

Early and judicious investments in real estate have added largely to his wealth. Realizing that without the development of home manufactures no city can thrive, his capital and encouragement have been extended to many well-known industries of the city and State, and while his ventures have not always been free from risk and ultimate loss, his foresight in these and other lines has brought him a fortune, variously estimated at from five to ten millions.

He has been ever ready to assist with his advice, his talents, and his money, all enterprises of a public nature looking toward the industrial or educational advancement of that city. Mr. Pratt has held no public office, except when acting as one of the Finance Commissioners for that city, to which important post he was elected in 1877 by the City Council. This honor was the more marked as he was not a member of the political party then in power. He is said to have been the leader in formulating the financial policy of that city. As his private interests pressed him for time, he resigned this office, but was again elected during Mayor Hodge's administration, emphasizing the respect of the City Government for his talents and financial ability, and affording a happy example of the non-partisanship that allows a body of one political color to recognize the merits of an opponent as well as the feeling of public spirit that induced him to aid, with his advice and experience, in rounding out into a successful term of office the administration of another party.

During his residence of over sixty years in that city, he has been connected with many charities and educational institutions. He has evinced great interest in the Maryland Institute for the promotion of the Mechanic Arts. He donated to it the costly bell and clock in the tower of the Institute Building.

As President of the Maryland School for the Deaf and Dumb, at Frederick, and of the House of Reformation for Colored Children, at Cheltenham, Prince George County, he has given much of his time and contributed largely of his private means toward their support.

While acting as Treasurer of the Peabody Institute, he handled the millions entrusted to his care with such good judgment that he was warmly praised by its founder, that eminent philanthropist, Geo. Peabody, who thought him one of the ablest financiers he had ever known.

To this trust, perhaps, we may look for one of the elements that contributed to the formulation of his plan to found an institution that will be a monument to his memory as well as a blessing to his people.

In his public bequests he did not forget the

home of his birth. In 1867, he endowed an
academy in North Middleborough, Mass.,
with the sum of $30,000, making it free to
children in a restricted territory.

In January, 1882, he communicated to the
Mayor and Council of the city of Baltimore
his purpose of building, at a cost of $225,000,
a library building, to be deeded, upon its
completion, with its site, to the city, and
then to deed a further sum which, with the
buildings and grounds, would amount to
$1,058,000, upon the condition that the city
should pay $50,000 annually forever as an
annuity for the support of the institution.

The City Government speedily accepted
his proposition and conditions, and after
such State and city legislation as was necessary for the accomplishment of the design, it
was ratified by a vote of the citizens of Baltimore. By taking these steps during his
life, instead of leaving the fund in the shape
of a bequest to be handled, according to the
judgment of trustees, and subject to suits,
delays, and possible final diversion from its
proper channel, Mr. Pratt has been able to

supervise all the plans, pay out to the best advantage all its moneys, and bring the scheme to a successful consummation during his life. As President of the Board of Trustees, it is hoped he may be able to supervise the actions of that body for many years.

In addition to the Central Library Building, on Mulberry Street, five sub-libraries have also been built in different parts of the city. The Board of Management was appointed by himself, and is self-perpetuating. His total gift amounted to $1,145,833, a larger sum than was at first intended. Of this amount, $833,333 was paid to the city, and, by his advice, was invested in city bonds until such time as the principal and accrued interest shall be capable of yielding the $50,000 per annum needed to add to the books of the library and for current expenses. In the meantime, this annuity is raised by a direct tax upon the city.

The parent building has a frontage of 81 feet and a depth of 140 feet, and is considered fire-proof. It is built of Maryland marble, in bold Romanesque style of architecture, with its characteristic semicircular forms, relief mouldings, embellishments and rich carvings. In the centre of the façade a tower rises to the height of ninety-eight feet. The front is adorned with allegorical designs. Its interior is finished in Tennessee and Irish marbles, plate glass and hardwood. It has a capacity of 200,000 volumes, and each of the sub-libraries a capacity of 10,000 volumes.

The libraries were opened to the public January 4, 1886. On January 1, 1888, there had been, after some years, a total registration of 55,551 names, and nearly 500,000 volumes were taken out during the year 1892. The central and sub-libraries employ a force of fifty-one people, and there are 122,770 volumes upon their shelves.

Mr. Pratt wisely provided that the management of the institution should be non-sectarian and non-political, and that neither religious nor political considerations should enter into its administration or the appointment of any of its officers or employés.

Mr. Pratt's large fortune is the result of tireless industry and fixedness of purpose. He confines himself to legitimate channels of trade and avoids all forms of speculation. Good fortune has not created in him vanity, nor have his good deeds begotten pride. In manner he is modest, quiet and unassuming. An eclectic in his religious views, he has long been an active member of the Unitarian Society of Baltimore.

As the founder of "The Enoch Pratt Free Library of Baltimore," the name of the subject of this sketch will be a household word in the city for all time. His gift being free to the residents of the city without reference to race, rank, or condition, his benefactions will enter the doors of a myriad of homes, offering to all, for the asking, the means of securing knowledge, of expanding their ideas, and of brightening their firesides.

The influence of such an institution is as gentle as the breath of spring, though its effects may not be at once apparent.

ROBERDEAU ANNAN McCORMICK.

LELAND STANFORD

LELAND STANFORD

"Some men are born great, some achieve greatness, and some have greatness thrust upon them." In the person of Leland Stanford, the subject of this brief review, it would seem that this trilogy of the world's advantages were centered.

Multi-millionaire, ex-Governor of the State of California, chief figure in the carrying out of probably the greatest mechanical project of its time—the building of the great Trans-continental Central Pacific Railroad; twice the recipient of the highest political honors at the hands of the citizens of his residential State, philanthropist and public educator, his name stands to-day before the people as the incarnation of the highest success attainable by the self-made man.

Leland Stanford was in every sense a self-made man, with an indomitable energy, a superlative sense of the necessity of toil and application, and the knowledge that, unaided by advantages, the successful American is dependent wholly upon his own efforts. This man builded for himself a reputation more than national and well-nigh world-wide.

Said Senator Stanford, in an interview dating some two years back : "To habits of bodily toil and the example of my father and his whole family, I place whatever credit attaches to my life." In this brief and modest summary of the causes which led to his extraordinary achievements in the social, political and philanthropic circles of this country, we find an admirable index of the character of the man with whom we have to deal.

Said Senator Stanford, in this same interview, and in relation to his birth and family: "I was one of seven brothers, six of whom preceded me to California, and I was the last to journey across the plains. I had but one sister, who died early in life. My pilgrimage to California occurred in 1852."

Probably no better example of the extraordinary sources from which may be traced the characteristic energy of Senator Stanford's after-life could be found than the following speech of his father's, which our subject was particularly fond of quoting: "'I am off for the woods, boys; all that are ready come along,' and we followed as we could." "There was one fellow," said Mr. Stanford, "who gave me a good deal of trouble by his steady method; he would drive his team right up to the wood pile, never lift his eyes off the box or seat, and go to the end of that wood pile and begin. When he lifted his eyes, the last stick of wood would be in the wagon. At fifteen I could not keep up with him; my back and shoulders would give out. At seventeen he could not keep up with me."

In this straightforward story of his early life, one who reads between the lines may probably find sufficient proof that Leland Stanford was born with the first element of greatness.

From the very hour of his arrival in what, in those distant days, was looked upon as the land of golden promise, Senator Stanford began the achievement of the greatness which no fair-minded critic can deny him. His association with the majority of the greatest enterprises of a time when enterprises of gigantic moment were of every-day occurrence, all Californians are familiar with.

Probably from the standpoint of achievement, the part that he played in the conception and carrying out of the stupendous plan of bridging the waste plains with railroad ties, and so to open up to the gifted locality he had chosen as his future home, the advantages of contact with the greater civilization of the East, is his most conspicuous success. While other men of equal financial prominence stand conspicuous as promoters of the great Central Pacific Railroad scheme, it is unquestionable that to the energy, intelligence and stability of Leland Stanford was chiefly due the carrying out of the enterprise which placed the western and the eastern shores of the Republic in perfect conjunction.

For thirty years Leland Stanford occupied the most prominent position in the management of the affairs of the great railroad system of the far West. This enormous railroad system, throughout which his influence was unceasingly felt, numbers some twelve thousand employés, and is more than seven thousand miles in length.

His interest in the welfare of the State which so often honored him, became a byword among its citizens. He was one of its greatest land-owners, one of the greatest patrons of its public enterprises, one of the most whole-souled and generous benefactors of its institutions. He was the largest owner of grape-growing lands in the world, the output of his enormous vineyards being close on to two million gallons of wine per year.

As the owner of real estate, there was probably no more successful operator of his time. All his holdings of real property in San Francisco, and throughout the State, have appreciated in value to an extraordinary extent.

As a patron of the "sport of kings," no man was more prominent in his day than Stanford. His superb stock and breeding farm at Palo Alto, has been the birth-place and home of some of the greatest race horses this country has ever known.

He was one of the first of the many great millionaires of California to build a residence worthy of the fortune which he attained. His home on the crest of Nob Hill, the fashionable quarter of San Francisco, while simple in architectural design, was of extraordinary beauty in its internal luxury and decorations. Rare and valuable specimens of statuary and paintings, tapestry and antique carvings, as well as valuable collections of various kinds, adorned the interior. In point of situation the "Governor's" home was as beautiful as any town residence in the world. It overlooked well-nigh all the scenic beauties so lavishly bestowed upon the environs of the city.

Last, but in no sense least, of the great good that Senator Stanford achieved, must be mentioned his endowment, generous without degree, of an institution of education that is certainly destined to take its place in the first rank. There is probably no more pathetic incident in the career of a man of equal prominence than that which directly brought about the founding of the splendid University at Palo Alto.

Senator Stanford was married to the daughter of Dyer Lathrop, of Albany, New York. For eighteen years this continuously happy association had no issue, but in 1868 there was born to the long-waiting parents a boy, in whom was centered every interest, hope, and ambition of the then already successful capitalist. What had by this time become the ruling ambition of the Senator's life was destined to be of brief duration. Sixteen years after his birth this only child died of typhoid fever in Italy.

One of the most interesting stories told of Senator Stanford in connection with his founding of the University of Palo Alto, is the statement, many times repeated, that he firmly believed that the boy in his dying hour, although widely separated from his father, said to him, "Father, don't say you have nothing to live for, you have a great deal to live for;" and so, from that hour, both Senator Stanford and his devoted and philanthropic wife determined that, as a fitting monument to the memory of their only child, the youth of California should benefit by the advantages of as liberal and well-endowed an institution of learning as could be found in the country.

The Leland Stanford, Jr., University is the youngest of our great institutions of learning. Probably no college or university has ever been favored with so generous an endowment at its inception, or so liberally supported and encouraged in its growth as this "Junior" of all our great Universities. Situated at Palo Alto, in the very heart of San Mateo County, and but an hour distant from the city of San Francisco, it enjoys almost every known advantage of climatic and scenic charms.

The grant of endowment, which was made mutually in the names of the Senator and his wife, was signed in November, 1885, and consists of 7,300 acres. In addition, the University is endowed with the following landed property, destined some day in its increased value to add phenomenally to its wealth: the Vina ranch in Butte and Tahama Counties, comprising 55,000 acres and including the largest vineyard in the world, some 4,000 acres in extent, and the Gridley ranch in Butte County, comprising 21,000 acres. Added to these enormous estates, a sufficient amount in money was contributed to place the institution at the start with a sum of $20,000,000 to its credit. The major portion of the residue of his estate and that of his wife will also ultimately fall to the University.

The grant of endowment sets forth that the nature of the institution shall be "that of a university, with such seminaries of learning as shall make it of the highest grade, including mechanical institutes, museums, galleries of art, laboratories, and conservatories, together with all things necessary for the study of agriculture in all its branches, and for mechanical training and the studies and exercises directed to the enlargement and cultivation of the mind."

The object of the institution is to qualify students for personal success and direct usefulness in life, to promote the public welfare by exercising an influence in behalf of humanity and civilization, teaching the blessings of liberty regulated by law, and inculcating a love and reverence for the great principles of government as derived from the inalienable rights of man to life, liberty and the pursuit of happiness.

Senator Stanford many times clearly stated that it was primarily his desire to establish and maintain at this University an educational system which would, if followed, fit the graduate for some useful pursuit, and to this end to cause the pupils, as early as may be, to declare the particular calling in life which they may select. It is distinctly stipulated that the trustees are to prohibit sectarian instruction, but that in the University there shall be taught a belief in the immortality of the soul, the existence of an all-wise, omnipotent Creator, and that obedience to His laws is the highest duty of man.

The University proper consists of three separate groups of buildings, each enclosing a large and separate quadrangle. The main quadrangle is 600 feet long and 250 feet wide, and about it are grouped twelve one-story buildings. These are really separate structures but so arranged as to be parts of one harmonious whole.

One of the most noticeable architectural features is the memorial arch, a splendid structure 80 feet in height by 86 feet wide and around the upper portion of it, in bas-relief, is an allegorical representation of the history of California. On either side of the arch are to be found the art gallery, the library and other buildings. These are two stories in height and contrast strongly with the general appearance of the squat style of early mission architecture which pervades the entire scheme.

In the early history of California, Senator Stanford played a prominent part in its somewhat erratic social and political conditions. Later on he was elected with enthusiastic acclaim to the Gubernatorial chair. In 1884, he was elected United States Senator as the representative of the Republican party, despite the fact that the Legislature was then considered distinctly Democratic, and, likewise, that the majority of the newspapers of San Francisco were opposed to his candidacy.

His entire career during his first Senatorial term stamped him in the eyes of the whole people as a legislator of the broadest views and essentially as a man of the times. He proved himself not only a shrewd and keen judge of human nature but also a man who held as first in importance the home welfare of his constituents. He showed throughout his term in the Senate a deep and kindly sympathy with the efforts of the thousands of ambitious settlers of the vast locality to which he himself had gone as a pioneer.

As an admirable index to his qualities, and as evidence of the broad theory of beneficence to which he held, it may not be inappropriate to quote from one of his most celebrated speeches: "Money is a force. It is the force that underlies our civilization and pushes it to the greatest possible activity. When it shall be understood that money is to be issued by the Government for the benefit of the great class of producers who demand it for industrial purposes, and that it is not created for the benefit of usurers to sweat it, and of gamblers to risk it, and of misers to hoard it, of millionaires to accumulate it, and of spendthrifts to distribute it in the gratification of their luxurious tastes, then some of the errors which now prevail in the financial system will have been dissipated, and the use of money much better understood."

Senator Stanford's resolution, introduced some three years since, petitioning the Government to advance money to the holders of real estate requiring this money for the development thereof, is the most powerful plea for the betterment of the farming class that has ever been introduced in this country.

His record as a second-term Senator is too recent to need reviewing here. The position which he continued to occupy as the enthusiastic promoter and earnest advocate of his Land Loan Bill gave him a prominence well-nigh international both as philanthropist and as statesman. He held that the land in which we live is by Nature fully endowed with riches, and that application, coupled with education, are the only requirements to the obtaining thereof. To such an extent had his interest in our agricultural population endeared him to that great multitude, it may be said that any honor which could have been bestowed upon him by the Populist party of the far West could have been his.

At the close of the session of Congress, in the spring of 1893, he returned to his home at Palo Alto. For several years disease had been making inroads upon his vitality, and on June 20, 1893, at the age of sixty-nine, his earthly career was ended. His name will be perpetuated in the noble institution which he established, and his memory will be cherished by the multitudes whom he befriended.

GEORGE PATRICK BRADY.

MARSHALL FIELD

MARSHALL FIELD

MARSHALL FIELD is called good-looking by those Chicago people who know the leading dry-goods merchant of the world, and who see in the quiet, gentle face, close-cut iron-gray hair, and short, dark mustache, lines of character-beauty. Like his close friend and Prairie Avenue neighbor, Philip D. Armour, he is the product of farm life in the East. He was born at Conway, Mass., in the harvest time of 1835, and had for a father the most intelligent and progressive farmer in the Bay State. Marshall never made much of a farm hand. He failed to see any fun in hustling after a plow or chasing the new calf in the pasture. His nature was too fine for such things, his thinking powers too deep and logical to be wasted on the drudgery of the farm. As boy and man he has always been of rather slight, delicate build, although possessing splendid health. Modest as a girl, he is very much averse to notice in the public prints, and while his name is as familiar on the tongues of Chicago people as the name of Clark Street, he probably has a smaller list of personal acquaintances than nine out of ten men doing business in a large city.

Mr. Field finished his education at Amherst, under the learned direction of his noted uncle, Dr. Nash, and began business life as clerk in a small dry-goods store at Pittsfield, Mass., receiving $6 per week salary. Last year his firm sold upward of $70,000,000 worth of goods. Pittsfield was not big enough or good enough for Mr. Field, and he speedily discovered that Chicago was his town. He became a regular out-and-out drummer for the pioneer dry-goods house of Cooley, Wadsworth & Co., and was a travelling comrade of Edson Keith, now his almost daily dinner companion at the millionaire's table of the Chicago Club. In 1862, he became a member of the firm of Cooley, Farwell & Co., and on December 20, 1864, the firm of Field, Palmer & Leiter was formed, Potter Palmer putting in most of the money, with Marshall Field and Levi Z. Leiter to run the business. The spring of 1865 brought the close of the war and the greatest depression ever known in the drygoods trade. The shrinkage was terrible, and young Field met his match in a most discouraging business situation. While not exactly repenting his venture in Chicago, he thought it was at least questionable, in a wise business sense, and to properly consider the matter, far removed from the scene of his trouble, he went to Europe. The fall of 1865 brought business activity to the country and lifted the dry-goods trade to the top round of prosperity, and Marshall Field was on hand all right. In 1867, Potter Palmer dropped out, and the firm became Field, Leiter & Co., changing again, by the retirement of Mr. Leiter, to Marshall Field & Co., in 1881, where it stands to-day as the greatest mercantile house in the world.

Harlow N. Higinbotham, President of the World's Fair, is Mr. Field's principal partner.

The Chicago fire of 1871 found Marshall Field's firm worth $5,000,000 of property of all kinds, insured for $3,500,000, of which it finally managed to win back $250,000. Before the smoke had died away over the ruins of his two houses, Mr. Field resumed business in the old car barns, nearly two miles distant from the business heart of the city. Then the big retail house, corner of State and Washington Streets, was rushed up, and a wholesale home of plain red brick and ugly iron shutters was built at Market and Madison Streets. To the retail store, building after building has been added on the State Street side, and now the magnificent annex at Wabash Avenue and Washington Street is nearing completion. The old wholesale house is used for stock storage, while business is carried on in a grand red granite block, eight stories high, covering an entire square of ground in the wholesale district. It is barren of the slightest attempt at ornamentation and is as severe in appearance as it is imposing in dimensions. Its total cost, furnished ready for business, was $1,280,000. In this building about 1,300 men are employed among the various departments, while in the retail store, nearly 2,000 men and women find work in plenty. In 1865, Mr. Field's firm did a business aggregating $8,000,000; in 1892, the figures leaped to $70,000,000. Mr. Field is the heaviest importer in America and pays cash.

In his quiet way, Mr. Field is a hard worker. Eight o'clock in the morning finds him at his desk in the wholesale house, which he leaves at 11 o'clock, going to the retail house for one or two hours, then to lunch at the Chicago Club, and later in the afternoon finishing the day's task at his desk in the red granite pile. During pleasant weather a quick drive down Michigan Boulevard, in a very ordinary sort of a buggy, behind a team of far from beautiful horses, is the prelude to supper and evening at home. And no man loves his home more than this clear-eyed, soft-voiced millionaire, who has Fortune for a hand-maid and Marshall Field, Jr., for a son. Young Marshall is happily married and settled in a home of his own close by his father's house, and is also interested in the wholesale branch of the firm. His daughter, Ethel, is the beautiful young wife of Judge Lambert Tree's son. Mrs. Field, Sr., was Miss Nannie Scott, daughter of an iron founder in Ironton, O., when kindly Fate gave her to the best of husbands. She is inclined towards society and gives quite a number of parties during the year. Mrs. Field is also active in all the works that interest women of big heart and wealth in great cities. Her charities are very widely expended.

Marshall Field's wealth has always been a source of much guessing among newspaper writers, club men and business men. To place it at $30,000,000 is probably far within the bounds of truth, and Mr. Field is known to possess $15,000,000 worth of gilt-edge business real estate outside of his dry-goods enterprise, and is a heavy investor in Chicago, Rock Island and Pacific, and other railroad stocks, in the manufacturing town of Pullman and in Pullman's Palace Car Company, besides interests in the Merchants' Loan and Trust Company and other banks.

As a generous giver to the cause of popular education, Mr. Field stands next to John D. Rockefeller. To Mr. Field the University of Chicago is indebted for the greater part of the magnificent site it is occupying as fast as the buildings can be erected. The land is worth $600,000, and to this gift he added the first $100,000 received toward the building fund. How much more Mr. Field has given or will give to this splendid educational scheme is at present a secret. No man ever learns Mr. Field's intentions in advance, and never, save by accident, or the betrayal of confidence, is the public made aware of his charities. While in no sense a clam, this peculiarly reticent man possesses all the clam-like possibilities of keeping his own counsel. As a citizen, he is very much the same as in business, public spirited, progressive, liberal and prompt in action. As a member of the Union League Club, he is always in the front rank of men seeking the good of the city, and so in the Commercial Club, is first in generous help for business interests. He has neither rival nor enemy.

The Young Men's Christian Association owes much to "the dry-goods prince" (Mr. Field abhors this title), and the same is true of the Chicago Manual Training School, the Art Institute, Historical Society, Chicago Relief and Aid Society, and a large list of other public enterprises. They all count on fat checks from Mr. Field every year, but his name must never appear on the contribution lists. This is the invariable condition with every gift. The Fields are members of the Presbyterian Church, and have for a pastor the gifted Dr. Barrows. In his religion, as in everything else, Mr. Field is totally devoid of display, and perhaps his chief characteristic in this line is the fact that he supports a city mission, but what city mission his most intimate friends have never learned.

Mr. Field in politics departs from his straight-line method of business. He is classed as a Democrat with his friends Potter Palmer, J. W. Doane and Lambert Tree, but the fact of the matter is, he can out-mugwump Franklin MacVeagh, one of his club lunch cronies. He voted for Garfield, for Blaine and for Cleveland, and is a pronounced admirer of his neighbor, Walter Q. Gresham, whom Mr. Cleveland has honored with the first place in his cabinet. Mr. Field is a champion of pure municipal politics, but Chicago has never been able to inveigle him into her Mayor's chair, although a long line of movements has been organized for that purpose. He is very willing that any one of his Democratic-Republican-mugwump friends should be Mayor, and he is also willing to soothe their pathways and sustain their administrations, but he drops politics at this line. It is well-known that Marshall Field would not accept the Presidency of the United States even if presented on a golden salver studded with rubies.

Behind the cold business mask of Marshall Field there is a good-natured man, fond of his cigar, genial to his friends, and possessed of a fair fund of humor. Twelve years ago the writer was an almost daily visitor as a newspaper reporter to Mr. Field's private office in the wholesale building, and so came to know him as a man of sensitive nature, an admirer of the great Chicago dailies, and numbering among his friends half-a-dozen reporters. His office was inside of a partition some seven feet high with entrance guarded by a vigilant private secretary. One day the writer hastened to Mr. Field in quest of some important information and found a new secretary on duty. Oh, yes, Mr. Field was in all right, but nobody could see him; busy, you know. All the reportorial blandishments failed to impress Mr. Secretary. In desperation the visitor presented a card and in a not patient tone of voice, exclaimed: "Just let Mr. Field cast his eagle eye over that card." Mr. Secretary was properly shocked. From over the top of the partition came a soft drawl: "Suppose you let me cast my eagle eye on yourself." The next hour was passed by a poverty reporter and multi-millionaire in a happy visit, the memory of which, recalled many years after, leaves Marshall Field anything but a cold, proud man.

Glancing over the hundreds of men in the wholesale department yesterday, the writer saw a splendid display of bright young faces. Scarcely an employé in the building could boast of forty years of life, and gray hairs were not in line at all. With scarcely an exception, every man in a responsible position has grown up with the house, has won his spurs by merit, and in a number of cases the spurs carry from $10,000 to $30,000 per year salary with them. It is in a great measure true of Marshall Field & Co.'s employés that they "are raised in the house," and among them the great merchant has found his most loyal friends and ablest counsellors.

No man ever called Marshall Field "Marsh." Just why this is true may prove food for the people who love to select one point about a man's character and weave to their satisfaction an estimate of him from his mother's knee to "dust to dust."

CHARLES M. FAYE.

John B. Gordon, Prest.

JOHNS HOPKINS.

DURING the war of 1812 there lived in Anne Arundel County, Md., a boy about fifteen years of age, who was destined to become the greatest financier his native State had ever known and whose name would be handed down to a grateful posterity as a national promoter of the great cause of education and philanthropy. He came of sturdy, upright and industrious Quaker stock. His ancestors settled in Maryland in the early days of the colony. Johns Hopkins University and Johns Hopkins Hospital are twin monuments for all time to the work and worth of their founder.

Mr. Hopkins' first experience in life was on his father's plantation. Tobacco was the main crop, and although it specially required slave labor in those days to make it remunerative, the Hopkins family, true to their conscience, freed their negroes in the latter part of the last century. Slave property was rated high, and when it is remembered that the Hopkins negroes numbered upwards of a hundred, it will be seen that the family made a genuine sacrifice for conscience sake. While most of his early days were spent in the tobacco fields, Johns Hopkins managed to find enough time to secure a moderate education. An incident that occurred about this time indicates the development of his mind for business. The story was often told by himself with zest.

During the war of 1812 the farmers of his part of the State, who marketed their crops at the historic city of Annapolis, found themselves in great straits. Relying in the main upon tobacco, for which they could not find any buyers, owing to the presence of the English fleet of war-ships, they found their credit with the city merchants exhausted. Mrs. Hopkins, the mother of Johns, took counsel with her boy, and at his suggestion gave him twenty turkeys to take to Annapolis, in order that he might purchase with the proceeds of their sale some tea and groceries. While Johns was trying to dispose of the turkeys, one of the roughs who infested the city at that time, snatched a gobbler and took to his heels. Johns Hopkins immediately made after him, but the chase was fruitless. On his return, however, he found that another rascal had made away with three more turkeys. He took the situation philosophically and decided that he would let them go with the other rather than run the risk of being robbed of any more.

"Now," Mr. Hopkins used to say, when he related the incident, "that was the most valuable lesson I ever learned in my early or even my later life. It taught me to take care not to lose the dollars in trying to save the cents."

When about eighteen years old, Mr. Hopkins was apprenticed to his uncle, Gerard T. Hopkins, in Baltimore, who conducted a well-known grocery establishment. The uncle was an earnest member of the Society of Friends, and devoted much of his time to travelling over the country preaching. He spent six months in an evangelistic tour among the Indians. All this while Johns was mastering the details of the business; so much so that when his uncle returned, Johns remarked to him:

"I fear, uncle, that unless thou spendest more time with thy business and less in the meeting houses, thy affairs will be in a sad condition."

"What!" exclaimed the uncle, who supposed himself to be possessed of a comfortable fortune. "Such impudence! Thou hadst better look to thy own affairs and not meddle with what thou knowest nothing about."

But Johns, young as he was, knew the situation better than his old uncle, though his warning passed unheeded. A few years later, the uncle went to the wall. Then Johns, in 1819, started in the grocery business with another young man, named Benjamin P. Moore. The young merchants had little or no cash capital, but such a high reputation for capacity and integrity had Johns Hopkins already earned, that they had no difficulty in establishing a good credit. The partnership ran three years, when it was dissolved, Mr. Hopkins taking with him his two younger brothers. The firm of Hopkins & Brothers had a most prosperous career, securing a large and very profitable Southern as well as local trade. Mr. Hopkins then laid the foundation of a fortune which at his death was estimated at from $8,000,000 to $10,000,000.

Mr. Hopkins retired from the grocery business in 1847, and thereafter devoted his thought and energy to a larger field of operations. He became a Director in the Baltimore and Ohio Railroad, in the management of which he took an active part until his death, which occurred on December 24, 1873, in his seventy-ninth year. His holdings of Baltimore and Ohio stock amounted to 17,000 shares, exceeded only by that held by the State of Maryland, which had contributed liberally to the road in its early days. On several occasions prior to 1857, the Baltimore and Ohio would have gone into bankruptcy had it not been for Mr. Hopkins, who had great and abiding faith in the road's future, and without hesitancy endorsed its notes to tide it over critical periods. On one occasion the road wanted to borrow $500,000. It drew its note, had it endorsed by Mr. Hopkins and sent an agent to a New York bank to raise the necessary cash. The agent had a conference with the bank officials, who examined the paper, but shook their heads, with the remark that they could not see their way to accommodate the Baltimore and Ohio. It happened that an old gentleman, who was reading a newspaper, overheard the conference, and when the agent from Baltimore started for the door with a very long face, the old gentleman dropped his newspaper and followed him. Tapping the latter on the shoulder, he said:

"Young man, did you say that paper was endorsed by Johns Hopkins?"

"Yes, sir," was the reply.

"Well, just you come along with me. I don't know anything about your railroad, but I do know Johns."

The agent came back to Baltimore with the $500,000 he went after, thanks to the confidence had in Mr. Hopkins.

When the panic of 1873 swept over the country, Johns Hopkins' strong hand again came to the rescue of the Baltimore and Ohio. He furnished it with $900,000 in cash, thus enabling it to pay its interest in cash, while other great roads were issuing certified checks or scrip. Nor was the railroad the only interest which he protected in those trying times. He practically controlled the banks of the Monumental City. He was for years President of the Merchants Bank and a Director of the first National, the Mechanics, the Central, the National Union, the Citizens and the Farmers and Planters. Besides this he was a Director of the Baltimore Warehouse Company, of the Mutual Marine Insurance Company and a large stockholder in the George's Creek Coal Company and Merchants and Miners

Steamship Company. His interests were almost identical with the entire business interests of Baltimore.

"This is a tornado," Mr. Hopkins exclaimed, when the news of the panic was brought to him in his office. For a moment excitement seized him. But it was only for a moment. A few hours later the Clearing House met, and by that time he had fully made up his mind what course to pursue. He had sized up the situation with Napoleonic skill, and his self-confidence restored the drooping courage of his associates. He told them that he "would put his shoulders to the wheel;" that he held $2,000,000 of commercial paper and large investments, all of which were affected by the crisis. He was prepared, however, he said, to devote his money and influence to avert the panic from Baltimore's business community. This announcement gave renewed confidence in Baltimore financial and commercial circles. Next morning he set out to do what he had proposed. He loaned his money until that was exhausted and then he loaned his name, which it was conceded was "as good as a bank note." In many instances he even charged nothing for his endorsement. It was then that Mr. Hopkins singly and alone checked the tide of disaster which was sweeping over New York, Philadelphia and other cities, but which, through his masterly action, was felt only indirectly in Baltimore.

The Johns Hopkins University, destined to be the central institution for higher education in this country, was in contemplation by Mr. Hopkins many years before his death. Such was also the case with the superb and complete hospital which bears his name and which had attracted the attention of medical men, not only all over America, but also in Europe. The University was incorporated in 1867, but the trustees did not begin the work of establishment until 1874, after Mr. Hopkins' death, when they elected Dr. Daniel C. Gilman President, an office which he still fills with honor and great credit. The work of instruction began in 1876, since which time it has grown with remarkable rapidity

Students no longer find it necessary to seek German or English Universities for opportunities and facilities for the most advanced work in science or literature. Since 1878, 841 persons have received the B. A. degree, while that of Doctor of Philosophy has been conferred on 249, most of whom were graduates of Harvard, Yale and other prominent institutions.

Mr. Hopkins left about $4,000,000 to the University, consisting largely of Baltimore and Ohio stock, valued then at about $3,000,000 and his large suburban estate, Clifton, which is held at about $1,000,000 more. He provided that only the interest should be used, thus maintaining the capital intact. When the Baltimore and Ohio Railroad in 1889 ceased paying dividends, the University found itself cramped for resources, but liberal friends came to the front and its prosperity was unimpaired.

To the hospital Mr. Hopkins left about $3,000,000, consisting of the finest warehouse property in Baltimore and his bank stock which formed a very considerable proportion of his gift. The hospital is one of the most interesting objects to visitors in the Monumental City. In construction and equipment it has not its superior in the world. Its location on the crest of Broadway Hill is magnificent. The grounds around it contain fourteen acres. The elevation is about 120 feet above the waters of the Chesapeake Bay. The scene from the tall dome is a panorama of beauty. Nearly fifteen years were consumed in its construction and all that art and science could give to attain perfection was brought into service. The heating and ventilating systems are in themselves marvels. By them each individual in a ward is supplied with at least one cubic foot of fresh air every second, of such a temperature as to give rise at no time to a feeling of discomfort. Doubtless, could Mr. Hopkins return and see the giant strides made by the institutions which owe their existence to his beneficence, he would feel that his fondest dreams had been far more than realized.

Mr. Hopkins' main characteristic was his

nerve. None but a man of nerve would have dared to do what he did during the panic of '73. Had he been a weaker man than he was, Baltimore would have experienced a financial crash that would have resulted in the collapse of almost every important commercial and financial enterprise within her borders.

"To what do you attribute your success in life?" Mr. Hopkins was asked by a friend, a few years prior to his death.

"To acting upon my intuitive judgment," was the great financier's reply. "When I hesitate too long in order to argue the question with myself or seek the advice of others, I almost always lose; but when I do what the first impulse suggests in an emergency, I succeed."

Mr. Hopkins left no successors, dying a bachelor. The public is his heir.

WILL J. GUARD.

CLAUS SPRECKELS

CLAUS SPRECKELS

THAT some great houses have been built on sand is proverbial, but in the subject of our biography this month we have to deal with the fame and fortune of a man built upon the even less stable substance—sugar. Claus Spreckels, the "Sugar King."

Men the world over have risen to eminence, earned great titles, and done great deeds in the achievement of their fortunes. To this one Hanoverian, however, can alone be given the credit of having amassed sufficient wealth in his adopted country to place him well in the front rank of its greatest capitalists, solely and directly through the profits that accrued from the growth and sale of sugar.

Not only has Mr. Spreckels a world-wide

reputation as the greatest sugar refiner and owner of sugar plantations on earth, but the enormous amount of money which is annually transferred to his ever-growing bank account places him in a position to enjoy what is probably one of the most extensive ready-money incomes in America.

As a citizen of California, the subject of this article takes rank as one of the most sincere and steadfast developers of the best interests of the great Pacific State. As a resident of San Francisco, where the major portion of his business is transacted and where many thousand employés have found engagement in the great sugar refineries which bear his name, Mr. Spreckels may well be mentioned as one of the most prominent and devoted citizens of the metropolis.

It is, however, in Hawaii that Claus Spreckels in very truth has earned the title "King." On these great Pacific Islands his enormous holdings, both in lands and buildings, and the employment of native labor, have made him the most conspicuous commercial figure. In addition to this distinction, the fact that a large portion of Mr. Spreckels' life is spent in Honolulu, where he is the possessor of a palatial residence, and is constantly engaged despite his far advanced age, in a personal supervision of the development of the crops which yield him such splendid financial result, make him likewise one of the best known and most admired residents of the former Kingdom.

It was in the year 1830 that there came to New York City from the low German countries a young immigrant, possessed of a minimum of the world's goods, coupled with a maximum of ambition and a well-ingrained appreciation of genuine application. From his native town of Hanover, where he was born of plain and frugal parents, the boy brought with him a masterful confidence in the opportunities which the new world opened up before him and which confidence the splendid results of his after-life have more than justified.

Like many others of his kind, the young man first started as a clerk in the ordinary

German "corner grocery." The years went by, and with his inherited frugality the clerk rose in his position, subsequently became a partner, and later on achieved what is ordinarily the limit of ambition in such cases and became the proprietor of a small retail grocery store in lower Church Street. He prospered as men of his kind and calibre must, and amassed, what to the ordinary man of similar origin, would have seemed more than a sufficient fortune upon which to retire and return to the always remembered and beloved Fatherland.

Not so in the case of Claus Spreckels, however. With scarcely any prominence and with a distinct desire to conduct his now extensive business operations with as little publicity as possible, he slowly became one of the most successful of the merchants of his special class. None of his successes seemed noteworthy, but the constant addition to his capital and the ceaseless application to his business, served to convince those who knew him well that the foundation of his stupendous fortune was already well begun.

He carried on enterprises of sufficient size and moment to have taxed the capacity and strength of well-nigh any corporation, but then as now he was to all intents entirely alone in the management of his affairs. He continued slowly but surely to gain ground in his adopted city until he became convinced that the keenness of competition and the restrictions of his capital forbade the further rapid development of which he was ambitious.

After some twenty years of assiduous activity in New York City, Mr. Spreckels emigrated to California, arriving there practically as one of its pioneers. He embarked once more in the retail grocery business. It was the period of rapid returns of large proportions for small investments, and his fortune grew apace. With his brothers, who had followed him from his native land, and, later on, to California, he purchased a controlling interest in a business which next to that of the vending of groceries seems most acceptable to the German commercial mind —the manufacture of beer. For $40,000 a controlling interest was obtained in the

Albany Brewery in San Francisco. The investment proved a most profitable one, and many dollars were added to the nucleus of the great Spreckels fortune.

As in the retail grocery field, however, it was not long before the practically limitless ambitions of the man found their restrictions in his new enterprise. During his grocery experience he had many times found great profit in speculation in sugar, and with his broad knowledge of this staple he was well fitted for the manipulation of its markets.

At the very outset of his investments in the sugar industry the wise judgment of the man was clearly demonstrated. He fully realized that the chief sources of supply were so far distant from the market in which he was most interested, that it was impossible for him to observe the fluctuations and the output. His one ambition was to control not only the sale of the staple, but the management of its source of supply. The West had given him success and fortune, and to the West he clung, although he went far beyond the then domain of his country. Down in the rich and fertile islands of the Southern Pacific Ocean he sought for fair fields for the growth of the succulent cane. Practically alone and in total ignorance of the then uncivilized country to which he journeyed, he began to build up what has since become the reigning industry of the Sandwich Islands.

Here, indeed, he found that Nature had been bountiful to a degree in the bestowal of her gifts. He saw the islands fertile, the climate suited in every way to his enterprise, and that, indeed, the great explorer Cook had chosen wisely when he named the group the "Friendly" Islands. So enormous were the opportunities offered by this new land that even the fabulous output of the mines of gold he had left behind him seemed almost insignificant. He realized immediately that sugar could be raised far more cheaply and of an equal quality with that of the Southern States, even when the cane was cultivated by the negro slave.

He found the natives and the simple monarch of the kingdom quite favorable to his enterprise, and the investment of his capital, which proved so profitable to himself, served for the subsequent development of the nationality. As might be well supposed, the success which he achieved caused many others to follow where he had led, but with the true genius of the financier, he managed to retain practically the sole control of the sugar output. He made money so rapidly that after a residence of but a brief period he in truth earned the world-wide title of "Sugar King of the Sandwich Islands." He was in truth king in more senses than one, for his enormous wealth yielded him influence surpassing that of the native monarch, Kalakaua. It is related as an example of his enormous wealth that the spendthrift king once borrowed from the Sugar Monarch the neat little sum of $1,000,000 to replenish his failing exchequer.

One of the primary secrets of his constantly growing wealth lay in the fact that every cane of sugar grown on his plantation was handled exclusively by himself, and shipped to the United States to refineries solely his own. At this time it was estimated that his yearly revenue exceeded $2,000,000. He controlled the entire sugar trade of the Pacific Coast, which amounted to five times that sum. It is stated that at this time his refineries turned out in the neighborhood of 700 barrels of sugar per day, and this, manipulated and sold under his direction, realized an approximate profit of $10 per barrel.

The Sugar Trust, the first of the great syndicates for the control of commercial interests, selected the Spreckels refineries for their opening assault. Overtures had been made to the great Sugar King for him to join in the advancement of the prices on this great staple, but without avail. As has been said before, however, Mr. Spreckels had always insisted in carrying on all his enterprises without outside assistance or interference. From the very outset he had built his fortune and his fame single-handed and alone.

His refusal to join the trust meant one of two things, either that he should be driven out of the field or that the enormous coalition should be forced to dissolve. With the characteristic courage which had served him so well throughout his life, he took up the fight; and, even against so powerful a foe, he sought no ally whatsoever. In the early part of this celebrated combat of dollar to dollar and mind to mind, the "King" realized that one of the first requisites of success in battle is for the general commanding to be in person upon the field of action. By this time, Mr. Spreckels was a man of greatly advanced age, but despite this fact, he left his island home and his San Francisco interests behind him and established himself on the very outskirts of the enemy's territory. Selecting Philadelphia as his base of operations, he purchased large properties there and upon them erected some gigantic refineries. The war was a long and bitter one, but the outcome of it is too recent to require but passing reference.

Of Mr. Spreckels' private life almost as much of interest could be related as of his public career. He married early in life a woman of extraction similar to his own. The great advancement in position which his enormous fortune led to has changed but little the simple character of either husband or wife. Mrs. Spreckels is noted for her many deeds of kindness and charity, carried on unknown to the outside world, among the people of her nationality. The "King" himself, while possessed of the grim ruggedness, partly his by inheritance and partly developed by an incessant struggle with the world, is, nevertheless, a man of liberal views and kindly disposition. He has always been known among his intimates as distinctly devoted to his domestic surroundings. The accumulation of his vast fortune has meant but little to him in the way of personal enjoyment, save in the knowledge of his practically limitless success.

Even to-day although the years have left their marks upon him, Claus Spreckels is still a man of exceptionally vigorous mentality with which a robust constitution has fully kept pace. He is a man of medium height and sturdy build. By this time his hair and beard which early in life had turned to gray, are patriarchal in their whiteness. The most striking characteristic of the man's otherwise stoical expression is the clearness and brilliancy of his blue eyes. One glance suffices to convince the observer of the exceeding shrewdness of mind which lies behind them.

Mr. Spreckels, like most men who have triumphed over their fellows in the fight for gain, has made many enemies—enemies so bitter that at times the newspapers have teemed with assault upon his character as a business man and virulent abuse of his business methods. Neither personal enmity nor journalistic antagonism have ever served, however, to make Claus Spreckels swerve one jot from the line of action, which in his belief led on to success.

In searching for a suitable motto to inscribe upon a tablet to the memory of the "Sugar King," one would find it difficult to select a better one than has been quite justifiably bestowed upon the city of Chicago —"I Will."

Even to-day, when the laurels of successful achievements are his, and when most men of his years would be more than glad to retire from the active field of incessant business controversy, Mr. Spreckels is as active in the development and carrying out of new enterprises as he was twenty years ago. He is constantly in transit, journeying yearly many hundreds of miles over sea and land and accompanied almost always by his devoted wife, who seems possessed of a well-nigh equal physical endurance. A large portion of Mr. Spreckels' time is spent in his superb home in the environs of Honolulu. His residence there, is the most sumptuous on the islands. Among the English, German, and American business men of the Island capital, Mr. Spreckels has many warm friends and associates. While he possesses also an extensive and comfortable home in San Francisco, Mr. Spreckels seems to prefer the marvellously attractive climate of Hawaii.

The Oceanic Steamship Company, which forms practically the only means of communication between the Islands and this country, is owned and controlled by Mr. Spreckels' sons, and the aged "King" is a frequent passenger upon the steamers of the line. At the slightest suggestion of business requiring his presence either in San Francisco or in the East, Mr. Spreckels, with an activity creditable to a far younger man- takes up his journey without the slightest hesitancy.

The enormous fortune which this old man has accumulated will, at his death, be divided among five children, four of whom are boys. The two eldest, John D. and Adolph, are prominent figures among the younger business men of San Francisco. They are both actively employed in the development of the Oceanic Steamship Company. Despite this fact, however, they find sufficient time to devote to many of the pleasures naturally sought after by men of their means and position.

Both the young men are enthusiastic yachtsmen and the joint owners of one of the crack schooners that hail from San Francisco. They are likewise liberal patrons of the turf, and while not owners of blooded horses or a racing stable, are as prominent as any in the racing affairs of the Pacific Coast. Both of them are thoroughly American in their tastes, and the elder, John D. Spreckels, has recently been credited with an ambition to become one of the leaders of the Republican party in California.

In the present political crisis in Hawaii, of which so much has recently been written, the Spreckels family has, considering its great interest in the Islands, been conspicuous chiefly for its rigid silence. All endeavors to obtain from the King himself an opinion upon the future of the land for which he has done so much, have signally failed. With the same reticence which has characterized his entire career, Mr. Spreckels prefers to remain a keen, but silent observer of the rapidly changing affairs of our neighboring state.

George Patrick Brady.

GEORGE M. PULLMAN

GEORGE M. PULLMAN

GEORGE M. PULLMAN's life-story, told in simplest English, reads like a romance, and to every young American must possess fascinating interest. From $40 a year to a fortune approximating $40,000,000 is one of the greatest strides ever accomplished. Mr. Pullman was born at Brocton, Chautauqua County, New York, March 3, 1831, and fourteen years later began his business career in a general store at Westfield, N. Y., working for his board and eighty cents a week. Three years as a clerk satisfied him that he was not cut out for that sort of trade and he joined his elder brother in the cabinet-making business at Albion, N. Y., to which place the family had removed. In a small way the Pullman Brothers struggled along until 1852, when their father died, and at the age of twenty-one George found himself the main support of his mother and five children of the family. The boy had never known the school days and boyhood pleasures forming so large a part of the happy memories of most men. Life was to him a serious problem, but the great load placed on his willing shoulders never caused him to stagger. The boy had a fixed purpose in life—the man still holds firmly to it. Make the best of your opportunities. Things did not go well with the Pullman family. A small cabinet-making business in a drowsy little country town could not feed and clothe half-a-dozen growing children, and George determined to abandon it after a number of very long and serious consultations with his mother, whom he loved devotedly and upon whose judgment he largely depended. George M. Pullman, boy and man, never ran fast, and so never stumbled in his enterprises.

Breaking away from the cabinet bench, he secured contracts from the State of New

York for the removal of warehouses and other buildings made necessary by the enlargement of the Erie Canal, and within a few years was able to make the family more comfortable and look with satisfaction on a bank account of $5,700. In 1859, Mrs. Matteson, of Chicago, whose husband was proprietor of the Matteson House, was visiting in Albion with her daughters, and in making his social visits young Pullman learned of the project then being agitated in Chicago, to raise the entire city eight feet, so as to enable the building of a sewerage system. His father had been a builder, and the gigantic feat of raising a city interested him so much that he finally decided to go West and see what the outlook was. Visiting Chicago and making a close examination of the field, he was finally led to offer his services to raise the Matteson House, one of the finest blocks in the city. He undertook the work and raised the hotel with the sidewalk, and all in such a way that business was not suspended nor the street blocked in any way. The feat at that time was so notable that it was the wonder of the city, and before he had finished the work of raising city blocks, the little capital brought from Albion reached $20,000 cash.

Then began the career that has made the name of Pullman famous the world over, and that has builded a beautiful city and made capable of earning eight per cent. a year one of the most gigantic industries in the world.

At Albion, he became acquainted with Senator Ben Field, a member of the State Senate, in 1854–56. Mr. Field was interested in legislation concerning sleeping-car fares, and the Woodruff Sleeping Car Company, in acknowledgment of his interest in their behalf, had given him the right to run their sleepers on a couple of Western roads. Mr. Pullman heard a great deal from his friend Field about the new car used for night service, and tells with relish the story of his first experience in a sleeper. He was making a journey of sixty miles and hearing that a night car was on the train he paid fifty cents for a berth in it, although he did not expect to use it. He wanted to see how the car looked. It had one bed near the floor, another two or three feet above it, and a third rising above the second. They were mere bunks, but they were the best sleeping accommodations that were provided at that time.

While Mr. Pullman was in Chicago raising buildings, he was called upon by Senator Field, with a request for several loans, and out of these accommodations an arrangement grew between them to run sleeping cars on the Alton road, Pullman to pay the Senator, who had secured the right to run the cars, half of the prospective earnings. Matters went on in this way for a short time, and meanwhile Field, who had no business tact, lost his sleeping-car service on the other two Western roads which had been given him. One day he came to Mr. Pullman and told him that he had an opportunity to buy back the privileges on the other roads, and that he would like to sell his half interest in the copartnership line to Mr. Pullman. A bargain was struck, and Mr. Pullman paid his partner $2,500. This was at the opening of the war, when the night trains on the Alton road had been taken off; the outlook for the Alton road was very dubious. It is a singular illustration of Mr. Pullman's good fortune that he had hardly concluded the purchase of his partner's half interest before business became so good that the night trains were started again and the sleeping-car business began at once to make returns. These sleeping-cars on the Alton road, with which Mr. Pullman's first experiments were tried, were simply two ordinary passenger coaches which he had changed into the commonest kind of sleeping-cars at slight expense. Fifty cents was charged for a berth, and the first night four berths were sold. About this time the Pike's Peak fever set in, and Mr. Pullman gravitated West and spent two or three years at Pike's Peak. He returned in 1864 and again took up his sleeping-car project.

In 1864, Mr. Pullman, who had been giving the sleeping-car business close attention, and who had become deeply interested in the thought that there was a wide field for inventive genius in that direction, met a master car-builder of the Alton Railroad, who was an old friend, and paid him $100 a month to take in charge the construction of a model car. He obtained the privilege of using a shed of the Alton Railroad in its yard at Chicago, and told the builder what sort of a car he wanted. The great question with him was how to have an upper and lower berth that would be comfortable. They were at that time the merest makeshifts to afford a night's rest. Mr. Pullman determined that the new car should be the handsomest ever made. Heretofore a sleeping-car had cost not more than $4,000 or $4,500. Looking the matter over and wondering how he could arrange two berths that would be roomy, comfortable and convenient, he was perplexed as to the disposition of the mattresses. At that time all the mattresses were put away in one section during the daytime. In fact, the early sleeping-cars were simply used for night cars, and not run in the daytime. Mr. Pullman's idea was to have a car that could be run on long trips either as a day or night car. With this object in view he started to build the "Pioneer." He found the mattresses could not be put on the floor because of the dust and discomfort. There was no place between the windows, and he finally said to his car builder, "Why not hinge an upper berth near the roof, and put the mattresses in it when the berth is closed during the daytime?" The car-builder replied at once that the car was not high enough and that the space would be too small. This was before cars were built with raised "decks," or roofs. "Then," said Mr. Pullman, "why not raise the car?" The outcome of this conversation was a direction that plans should be drawn for a car as wide and as high as would be necessary to get in two berths, including one hinged to the upper side of the car. The plan was accurately drawn for a car one foot wider and two and one-half feet higher than any car that had heretofore been built in this country.

Of course, the regulation railroad official laughed and sneered at the enterprise, but the man whose brain and courage had lifted a large part of Chicago out of the mud went on with his work and produced the "Pioneer," the first Pullman palace car, a model of comfort, safety and lavish decoration, at a cost of $18,000 and twelve months of patient labor. It was an immediate success. The assassination of Lincoln occurring at this time it was suggested that the "Pioneer" be used in the funeral train, and it was run from Springfield to Chicago on the Alton road. As had been predicted when the car was built, it was too wide to run on the roads as then constructed. It was necessary for the Alton road to send along its line and cut off the platforms that projected, and to make numerous changes at stations so that the car, with its width of an additional foot, could pass. When General Grant came home from the war, the "Pioneer" was used to carry him from Detroit to Galena over the Michigan Central, and the railroad was compelled to cut off depot platforms and make other changes in order that the car might pass. From that day to this, railroads have been built for Pullman cars as a feature.

Of Pullman's Palace Car Company, now housed in a magnificent $1,000,000 office building in Chicago, little need be said, beyond quoting some tremendous figures of millions. Up to 1867, Mr. Pullman conducted his business alone, but in that year organized a company with prominent railroad managers and acute business men as stockholders. In 1867, the capital stock was $6,000,000; 1881, $8,000,000; 1883, more than $13,000,000, and to-day more than $30,000,000. The annual output of manufactured products from the Pullman car works ranges from $12,000,000 to $14,000,000 in value. In the operating department more than 14,000 persons are employed, receiving annually about $8,000,000 in salaries. At the Pullman shops about 6,000 persons do the work and are paid nearly $4,000,000 per year, or an average of over $600 each.

The city of Pullman is one of the most beautiful in the world, and is the outcome of the heart and brain of the little dry-goods clerk of Westfield. To-day this magic city is within the limits of Chicago, in the Thirty-fourth Ward, and contains some 14,000 people and nearly 5,000 buildings; January 1, 1881, it was a stretch of bleak prairie ten miles south of Chicago limits. The Pullman Company invested $8,000,000 in this wonderful city before a penny was returned in earnings, and now, including the industries allied to the great Pullman car works, the enterprise pays 6 per cent. independent of the income of Pullman's Palace Car Company as a servant of the travelling public. Without a jail, without a saloon, a gambling place, or other "shady resort," the peerless little city has streets as fine as Chicago boulevards, beautiful parks, lawns, flowers, theatres, schools and churches, business men are prosperous and the working people happy in their model homes of pressed brick and perfect sanitary conditions.

What an object lesson to the young American of this fretful hurrying age!

George M. Pullman is one of the style of men popularly described as a "perfect gentleman." His sixty-two years of life have touched his kindly face lightly. He has been an extensive traveller in foreign lands, and is a very pleasant talker. No man ever had a more loyal and unselfish friend. The boy who loved his mother in Brocton is the husband and father who worships his family in Chicago. Mr. Pullman is a member of half-a-dozen Chicago clubs, a patron of art and music, and a "chum" of his neighbors, Philip D. Armour and Marshall Field.

The home of the Pullmans is on the lake shore, Prairie Avenue and Eighteenth Street, the corner of the lawn touching the spot where occurred the Fort Dearborn Massacre in the Indian days of Chicago, which Mr. Pullman has recently commemorated by a splendid bronze group. The house is of fine brownstone, and one of the most costly in the city, and the family is made up of father and mother; Florence, a beautiful brunette of twenty-two; Harriet, a duplicate of her mother, age twenty, and George M., Jr., and Sanger, twins, age sixteen, and the pride of George M. Pullman's every conscious hour.

Mrs. Pullman was Harriet Sanger, daughter of J. Y. Sanger, of Ottawa, Ill., where she was married to Mr. Pullman in 1867. She is a very lovely woman, and with her children is largely interested in works of charity. They have wards in hospitals and a fresh air enterprise for women and girls, besides being large contributors to general charities. In society, the Pullman ladies are leaders in the exclusive Prairie Avenue circles.   CHARLES M. FAYE.

PETER COOPER

PETER COOPER

WHEN one remembers that only ten years have passed since Peter Cooper's death, it is startling to hear him say, in one of his later addresses : "When I was born, New York contained 27,000 inhabitants. The upper limits of the city were at Chambers Street. Not a single free school, either by day or night, existed. General Washington had just entered upon his first term as President of the United States."

He was born in New York City, February 12, 1791. His mother has been described as a woman "in whom there was a rare blending of sweetness and fire, of force and tenderness." She was the daughter of John Campbell, a successful potter, who was an Alderman of New York, and Deputy Quartermaster General during the Revolutionary War. On his father's side, he was of English descent, and both grandfather and father served in the Continental Army, the latter rising to the rank of lieutenant.

At the close of the war, Mr. Cooper established a hat factory on what was then known as Little Dock Street, since become a part of Water Street. Here Peter was born. His father named him after the great apostle, because he believed he had been told to do so in a dream. Young Peter's early life was one of hardships. When he was three years old, his father moved his hat factory to Duane Street and Broadway, and as soon as the boy was old enough to work he was set at pulling hair from rabbit skins and cutting fur. He was very useful in the shop, and before he was fifteen years old was able to make every part of a hat. His father was not formed to achieve success in business, seeming to lack perseverance and ambition, and, becoming dissatisfied, sold out and removed to Peekskill, where he set up a small brewery, Peter's duty being to deliver the kegs of ale to the places in town and in the country where it was sold, and collect the empty kegs.

The results of this venture were discouraging, consequently there was a removal to Catskill. There his father opened a hat store and, besides this, engaged in the manufacture of bricks. Peter, who was older and stronger now, was made useful in carrying and turning them. This experiment, too, was unsuccessful; so the hat store was moved to Brooklyn. Not long afterward the family went to Newburg, and the father opened another brewery. Peter did not remain long here. He was now seventeen years old, and being ambitious, believed there were better opportunities for him in his native city, so he resolved to go there.

He had carefully saved up $10 of his earnings, and coming to New York, he saw, soon after his arrival, the advertisement of a lottery. He purchased a ticket, but drew— a blank. His $10 were gone, and he was penniless. Later in life he often alluded to this experience as being an excellent lesson —worth more to him than it cost.

For several days he walked the streets of the city looking for work. At last he found a carriage shop owned by Burtis & Woodward, at the corner of Broadway and Chambers Street. They were willing to accept his services if he would agree to remain with them until he should be of age. He was to receive twenty-five dollars a year and his board. The offer was accepted at once, and Peter started in to learn to be a carriage-maker. Of this period he said, in after years: "I spent all my spare time in ornamental carving, in an upper room which my grandmother gave me for this purpose. This was my occupation instead of walking the streets or going to places of public resort as did other apprentices of my age."

Here his inventive genius first asserted itself, and he began to see and remedy defects in the very tools he was being taught to use. The most important of his inventions, while an apprentice, was a machine for mortising the hubs of wagon wheels.

His employers were so well pleased with him that at the expiration of his time they offered to advance him the money to start in business on his own account. Peter, however, declined the offer because he had resolved early in life never to be in debt.

For a short time he followed his trade in New York City, then, removing to Hempstead, Long Island, he worked for a while in a woollen factory at a dollar and a half per day, and soon after invented a machine for shearing the nap from cloth. It was patented and had a rapid sale during the war of 1812, when woollen cloth was in great demand. It is interesting to note that one of the first purchasers of his machines was Matthew Vassar, the founder of Vassar College.

He soon had $500 saved up, and his prospects were bright, but learning that his father was in trouble, and under the pressure of debt, he applied his little savings to the most pressing debts, and arranged for the settlement of the rest, thus saving his father from bankruptcy.

On December 22, 1813, when twenty-two

years of age, he married Miss Sarah Bedel. She was a woman of rare qualities and a loving and devoted wife during fifty-six years of married life. She seconded every benevolent impulse, and made the fulfilment of his great scheme possible by her wise and resolute economy. After her death, Mr. Cooper said of her: "She was the day-star, the solace and inspiration of my life."

Six children were born unto them, four of whom died in childhood. The two surviving are the Hon. Edward Cooper and Mrs. Abraham S. Hewitt (Sarah Amelia Cooper).

With the declaration of peace and the renewal of the importation of British goods, the demand for the shearing machine ceased, but by turning his shop into a cabinetware and furniture factory, he placed it in salable condition and, finding a purchaser, moved to New York.

Here he started in the grocery business at Bowery and Pirington Street. One day, about a year after opening the grocery store, he met John Vreeland, the well-known hardware man, of whom he had bought tools when an apprentice in the carriage business. Vreeland remarked that there was a glue factory for sale on the Old Middle Road, and advised Peter to take hold of it. Acting on the suggestion he bought it, together with the unexpired lease of the ground for nineteen years. He knew nothing about the manufacture of glue when he started in, but soon was turning out the best glue in the country, and indeed an article superior to that which came from Ireland, and which previously was most in use, as the American glue was of poor quality. The manufacture of isinglass, oil, whiting and prepared chalk was soon added. The lease to this place having expired, ten acres on Maspeth Avenue, Brooklyn, were purchased, and here a factory was built to remain till the present day, with many improvements within and without.

In 1823, when the question was under discussion as to the best motive-power to be used upon the Erie Canal, then in process of construction, he made the experiment of employing an endless chain for the purpose. He had his idea patented, and at one time it seemed probable that it would be used upon the canal. It was, however, abandoned, probably "because mules voted, and the owners of mules had no use for an endless chain." His method of motive-power anticipated the modern mode of cable car propulsion by many years.

Industry and economy are the secret of his success. For twenty years he was his own bookkeeper, clerk and salesman, going to the factory at dawn to light the fires, and spending his evenings at home, posting his books, writing, and reading to his family.

By his success in the glue business, Mr. Cooper laid the foundation of his fortune. Now, indeed, "the boy had come to something." He had grown to be one of the most extensive business men of the country, with unlimited credit and surplus capital to invest in large enterprises.

In 1828, he was induced by two plausible gentlemen to make such an investment, namely, to unite with them in the purchase of 3,000 acres of land within the city limits of Baltimore for $105,000. When the time came for the partners to pay their shares, it was found that Mr. Cooper was the only one who had the funds, and he finally acquired the whole property by buying out his partners.

This purchase occasioned Mr. Cooper's interest in the Baltimore and Ohio Railroad, and led to his construction of the first American locomotive, about which he says: "When I first purchased the property it was in the midst of a great excitement, created by a promise of the rapid completion of the Baltimore and Ohio Railroad, which had been commenced by a subscription of $5 per share. In the course of the first year's operation they had spent more than $5 per share. But the road had to make so many short turns in going around points of rocks that they found they could not complete the route without a much larger sum than they had supposed would be necessary; while the many short turns in the road seemed to render it entirely useless for locomotive purposes. The principal stockholders had become so discouraged that they said they would not pay any more, and would lose all they had already paid in. After conversing with them, I told them that if they would hold on a little while I would put a small locomotive on the road, which I thought would demonstrate the practicability of using steam engines on the road, even with all the short turns in it. I built a small engine for that purpose, put it upon the road, and invited the stockholders to witness the experiment. After a good deal of trouble and difficulty in accomplishing the work, the stockholders came. Thirty-six men were taken into a car, with six men on the locomotive, which carried its own fuel and water, and having to go up hill eighteen feet to a mile, and turn all the short turns around the points of rocks, we succeeded in making the thirteen miles, on the first passage out, in one hour and twelve minutes, and we returned from Ellicott's Mills to Baltimore in fifty-seven minutes. This locomotive was built to demonstrate that cars could be drawn around short curves, beyond anything believed at that time to be possible. The success of this locomotive also answered the question of the possibility of building railroads in a country scarce of capital, and with immense stretches of very rough country to pass, in order to connect commercial centres, without the deep cuts, the tunnelling and the levelling which short curves might avoid. My contrivance saved this road from bankruptcy."

In the same year, 1830, not being able readily to dispose of his 3,000 acres of land, Mr. Cooper determined to go into the manufacture of charcoal iron. He says: "In my efforts to make iron, I had to begin by burning the wood growing upon the spot into charcoal, and in order to do that I erected large kilns, 25 feet in diameter, 12 feet high, circular in form, hooped around with iron at the top, arched over so as to make a tight place in which to put the wood, with single bricks left out in different places in order to smother the fire out when the wood was sufficiently burned. After having burned the coal in one of these kilns perfectly, and believing the fire entirely smothered out, we attempted to take the coal out of the kiln; but when we had got it about half-way out, the coal itself took fire, and the men, after carrying water for some time to extinguish it, gave up in despair. I then went myself to the door of the kiln to see if anything more could be done, and just as I entered, the gas exploded and enveloped me in a sheet of flame. I had to run some ten feet to get out, and in doing so, my eyebrows and whiskers were burned, and my fur hat was scorched down to the body of the fur. I seemed to be literally blown out by the explosion, and I narrowly escaped with my life."

Mr. Cooper, however, did not remain in Baltimore to manage the iron works, though their future prosperity was now certain. He sold out to some Boston capitalists, who formed the Canton Iron Company. He took a large part of his pay in stock at a nominal value of $44 per share which he held until the shares were finally sold at $230.

Returning to New York City he erected a rolling and wire mill. At every step he discovered or applied some new idea, the most important being the successful application of anthracite coal to the puddling of iron, after many failures in other mills.

Trenton, N. J., was next the field of his operations. In 1845, he removed his machinery there and erected the largest rolling mill at that time in the United States. He also built rolling mills in Phillipsburg, N. J., and purchasing the Andover mines, built eight miles of connecting railway. He manufactured railroad iron, and was the first to roll wrought iron beams for fire-proof buildings.

Mr. Cooper's active mind was not alone content with the management of his business. He took a warm interest in local politics, and served in both branches of the New York Common Council. He was prominent in every movement for municipal improvement, memorably so in the hard struggle in carrying to success the Croton Aqueduct plans. Parallel with his efforts to "place a spring in every house," was another work with results equally lasting. The city was filled with children, who had not the opportunity of obtaining even a primary education. His ceaseless activity in this direction made it a matter of course that he should be named as one of the city's first Board of Commissioners of Public Schools, and to him is due in no small degree the completeness of the present public school system in New York.

His study of and work for a general school system led him to realize that it could not supply a technological education, and he determined to establish in his native city an institution in which the working classes could secure that instruction for which he, when young and ambitious, sought in vain; for the advantages of school were denied him. In his whole life he had attended only every other day for a single year.

With a clear perception of the city's future growth in population, he purchased the piece of ground bounded by Third and Fourth Avenues, Eighth Street and Astor Place. Here, in 1854, was laid the corner-stone of the Cooper Union for the advancement of science and art. The scroll placed in the corner-stone reads: "The great object that

I desire to accomplish by the erection of this institution is to open the avenues of scientific knowledge to the youth of our city and country, and so unfold the volume of Nature that the young may see the beauties of creation, enjoy its blessings and learn to love the Author from whom cometh every good and perfect gift." In 1859, the finished building was transferred in fee simple to a Board of Trustees, and with it a broad, liberal, well-endowed plan for the perpetual education of the young of both sexes, "in all branches of knowledge through which men and women earn their bread." The Cooper Institute contains free schools in art and design and furnishes free lectures, free reading-rooms and free libraries, containing works in science and art. Its total cost exceeded $750,000. It has an endowment of $300,000, and in addition realizes a good income from the rental of halls and part of the building for business purposes.

Last year 576,537 persons availed themselves of the Free Reading-room and Library. In the Women's Classes 285 pupils were admitted to the Free Art School; forty-nine to the Free Classes in Stenography and Type-writing, and thirty-two to the Free School of Telegraphy. The Free Night School of Science numbered 1,308 pupils, and the Free Night School of Art, 1,767.

The Faculty of Instruction comprises a large corps of men and women specially fitted for the work. The endowment fund, although large, is not sufficient to provide instruction and accommodations for the vast army of hungry seekers after knowledge that apply for admission. As bequests from other wealthy and philanthropic people are received, further provision is made for their accommodation. Already the noble example set by the founder of this institution has been followed by persons in other cities, and the circle is ever widening.

Honors unsought were showered upon Peter Cooper. He was at the head of three telegraph companies, was associated with Cyrus Field in the laying of the Atlantic Cable from America to Europe, and in 1876, was nominated by the National Independent party for the Presidency of the United States; but he died as he lived the same kindly, gentle, unostentatious, unselfish man.

Shortly before his death, he remarked: "My sun is not setting in clouds and darkness, but is going down cheerfully in a clear firmament, lighted up by the glory of God. * * * I seem to hear my mother calling me, as she used to do when I was a boy: 'Peter, Peter, it is about bed-time!'"

In looking after the interests of his great philanthropic work at the institution that bears his name, he contracted a cold which terminated in pneumonia, and which resulted in his death April 5, 1883.

For industry, honesty, thrift, frugality, indomitable perseverance, courage surmounting all difficulties, business tact, broad philanthropy, and a wise disposition of his wealth, few persons furnish examples so worthy of imitation by the aspiring young business man as the subject of this sketch.

CLIFTON R. BECHTEL.

CHARLES L. TIFFANY

CHARLES LEWIS TIFFANY

FEW prominent business houses in this country rest upon a more solid groundwork of honorable dealing than that founded by the subject of our sketch. The name of Tiffany & Co. stands for the best workmanship and the best materials, wherever that name is known.

Charles Lewis Tiffany was born at Killingly, Conn., February 15, 1812. His ancestors were among the early settlers of New England. His father, Comfort Tiffany, resided at Attleboro, Mass., where he married Miss Chloe Draper, and soon after removed to Danielsonville, Conn., where he engaged in the manufacture of cotton goods.

The war of 1812, by interrupting importations from abroad, gave a decided impulse to manufactures in this country, and for a time they seemed to flourish, being protected by the duty on foreign goods. But with the imperfect machinery then in use, and with the undeveloped state of cotton culture in the South, Comfort Tiffany's progress towards wealth was slow.

Charles Lewis, his eldest son, received his early education at the district school, and afterwards spent two years at the Plainfield Academy, then in charge of John Witter, a Yale graduate, and teacher of some note.

About this time his father, desiring to enter into manufacturing operations upon a larger scale, organized the Brooklyn Manufacturing Company, and began the erection of mills at Brooklyn, Conn., on the Quinebaug River. While these were in process of construction, he opened a small country store, and Charles, who was but fifteen years of age, was taken from school, and placed in charge. The business prospered and young Tiffany made repeated trips to New York to purchase goods. Early in his career he evinced great business sagacity and developed that high standard of honorable dealing which has since secured the confidence and esteem of the commercial world.

Soon after the completion of the cotton mill, Comfort Tiffany purchased his associates' interests, and, taking his son into partnership, conducted the business under the firm name of C. Tiffany & Son. Feeling that his education was very incomplete, Charles now spent several terms at the Brooklyn Academy, and then entered the practical school of business life. Here he soon showed that artistic taste which contributed so largely to his later success. In the choice of new patterns and in the adaptation of old ones, in the improvement of fabrics, and in wisely determining what would suit the popular taste, his ingenuity and his æsthetic sense contributed in no small degree to the success of the business.

But he felt himself possessed of qualities which claimed a larger field for their development. He had worked hard, but, so far, the remuneration had been small. Counselling with his father, he secured his consent to a dissolution of the firm, and the early summer of 1837 found the son seeking for employment in New York City. He sought out a former school-fellow, John B. Young, who had come to the city several months before, and who was employed in a stationery and fancy goods store. When we remember that the great panic of 1837 had just swept like a cyclone through the country, and that commerce was at a stand-still and the wheels of trade were stopped, we can imagine that they found the prospect anything but flattering. But with the undaunted spirit that young Tiffany possessed, it would have taken two panics piled one upon the other, to baffle him.

Accordingly, we find the two friends coolly canvassing the business possibilities. Mr. Young had acquired some knowledge of the fancy goods and stationery business, and Tiffany was not without ideas of his own. Each believed thoroughly in himself, and, at the same time, had the most unbounded confidence in the other. They were entirely without capital, but upon presenting their plans to Comfort Tiffany, which met with his approval, he promptly advanced $500 apiece to the young mercantile adventurers. With this capital they launched the firm of Tiffany & Young, and established themselves at 259 Broadway, opposite City Hall Park. This was regarded at the time as being much too far up-town, but the new firm found encouragement in the fact that a young and enterprising dry-goods merchant, named Alexander T. Stewart, was doing a prosperous business two doors farther on.

The building was an unpretentious one, with a frontage of only fifteen feet. This was quickly stocked with fine stationery, fancy articles, umbrellas, walking-sticks, cabinets, desks, dressing-cases, fans, leather-work, Chinese pottery, Japanese lacquer work, terra-cotta ware, and curiosities of every description. Mr. Tiffany's artistic taste more than made up for what the stock lacked in quantity. The selection of the goods had been made with admirable judgment, and their arrangement was in itself a work of art.

Grand openings, largely advertised, were unknown at that early day, but the 18th of September, 1837, found the little shop ready for customers, and the unusual attractions soon became the talk of the town. Each customer became a "telling" advertisement, for every one that saw the artistic display of goods found a pleasure in speaking of it to his neighbor. Fashionable shoppers, on their way to the larger establishments on lower Broadway, soon learned to drop in, and the courtesy with which they were received by the members of the new firm, and the attractive display of desirable goods, soon made of them regular customers. New Year's Day was the great day in New York for the giving of presents, and the receipts on the preceding day were $675. This culmination of an exceedingly busy and profitable holiday week gave great encouragement to the young firm.

From this time forward success seemed to be fully assured. Mr. Tiffany's constant effort was directed to the purchase of the very best goods in the market. The importations of the large houses were diligently searched for whatever might contribute to the reputation and advantage of the firm. Manufacturers and importers were glad to consign their goods to a house where their merits would be so attractively displayed.

The year 1838 closed most auspiciously for the house of Tiffany & Young, but on January 1, 1839, their sky was overcast with clouds. Knowing that the sales on the previous day had been very large, and supposing that the receipts would be found in the cash drawer, thieves broke in and carried off almost everything of value, but the cash was safe, having been taken home by the partners. The loss, which amounted to nearly $4,000, was keenly felt for a time, but did not interrupt their business.

In 1841, their growing business justified them in taking the next building. This increased their frontage on Broadway to forty-five feet, and gave them a fine show window on Warren Street. The unerring taste of Mr. Tiffany suggested additional attractions in the way of Bohemian glassware, French and Dresden porcelain, cutlery and clocks. Up to this time but little had been done in jewelry. That department had not been overlooked; indeed, it had received careful consideration, but the time was not quite ripe for the execution of their plans.

The firm name was now changed to Tiffany, Young & Ellis, and each member took charge of a special department, for which he made himself wholly responsible. The next move was a very important one. It had been the practice of this house from the first to consider every contemplated change very carefully, and after the plans had all been fully matured, to act with the utmost promptitude and decision. The manufactures of this country were still in their infancy. In many lines there was no competition with manufacturers abroad. Our merchants were wholly dependent upon the importers, and the importers had little choice in the character and quality of the goods sent them. It dawned upon the minds of the young firm that if they had opportunity to inspect the markets of Europe they could find goods of higher grade, and goods better adapted to the wants of the people. Accordingly, Mr. Young was deputed to go abroad, and after visiting the principal art and manufacturing centres, he returned with a rich store of really artistic goods, and succeeded in establishing valuable business relations with several of the leading foreign mercantile and manufacturing houses.

The results of Mr. Young's trip were soon made apparent in the rare and artistic display of goods. The house of Tiffany, Young & Ellis became a centre of attraction. The wealthy and cultivated people, when they met on the street, were accustomed to ask each other whether they had seen the latest imported novelty at Tiffany's. Not only the residents of the metropolis, but strangers visiting the city, were drawn thither. To visit New York City without seeing Tiffany's was like going to witness the play of "Hamlet" without seeing the Prince.

On November 30, 1841, Mr. Tiffany entered into a new partnership, but without dissolving the old. His marriage with Miss Harriet Olivia Avery Young, sister of his business partner, and daughter of Judge Young, of Killingly, Conn., was signally blessed. She was a woman of unusual beauty, of amiable disposition, and of most estimable character. Four sons and two daughters were born to them. Two of the sons died in childhood; a daughter and son are married, Annie Olivia (Mrs. Alfred Mitchell) and Louis Comfort; and Louise Harriet and Burnett Young Tiffany reside with their parents. Mr. Mitchell, Louis C. and Burnett Y. Tiffany are all associated with the firm. Mr. and Mrs. Tiffany celebrated their golden wedding, November 30, 1891. The noted gathering was held at the elegant mansion, occupied by his son on Madison Avenue, near Central Park. This imposing residence Mr. Tiffany built for himself, but concluding after it was finished that he and his beloved wife would feel more comfortable to spend their closing years in their old home, gave the new residence to his son.

Four years of concentrated effort, of enthusiastic ardor, of honorable dealing, and of improved business methods, had placed the firm of Tiffany, Young & Ellis in the van. As rapidly as the people became educated to the appreciation and enjoyment of a higher grade of goods, the finest establishments in London, Paris, Rome, and Florence were laid under tribute. The idea of Art Perfection, like a guiding star, controlled every step.

Ten years of uninterrupted success again found their quarters insufficient, and in 1847 they removed to the corner of Broadway and Chambers Street. The next year they began the manufacture of jewelry, and a large part of their importations ceased. Such was the rare taste of Mr. Tiffany that their manufactured products compared most favorably with the best imported articles, and they soon found themselves on the high road to the first place as a jewelry house in America.

From jewelry the step to precious stones and gems was easy and natural. Owing to the large values often embedded in very small stones, the growth of this branch of the business was at first slow, but Mr. Tiffany, with a discriminating and refined knowledge gained from close study in every department of art in which he had been engaged, a knowledge which it is difficult to understand, and still more difficult to explain, soon learned the peculiar charm and subtle fascination of each individual stone, and could advise its judicious treatment by the practical lapidary. So deep and intense was his innate sense of the "fitness of things" that whatever branch of the business came under his view, his æsthetic faculty at once perceived its art possibilities, and the highest results were soon achieved. Some men early reach their limit of attainment, but no heights seemed too steep or too lofty for Mr. Tiffany to climb.

"It is the unexpected that happens," and the sagacious business man is always prepared for it when it comes. The disasters of one business house often furnish opportunities to another. The misfortunes of one country frequently conduce to the commercial advantage of another country. In 1848, the political disturbances in France caused a rapid decline in the values of precious stones. Many wealthy people of Paris were obliged to sacrifice their jewels. Prices were forced down to half their former value. Mr. Tiffany at once took advantage of the depressed market; every available dollar was invested in Parisian diamonds, which were brought home and stored away until such time as there should be a demand for them. This movement evinced keen business foresight, and at once gave to the house the first place among dealers in precious stones in this country.

The inherent value of a gem is often greatly enhanced by its historic associations. Mr. Tiffany was no less quick to discover this value of a stone. When the zone of diamonds worn by the unfortunate Marie Antoinette was offered for sale, Mr. Tiffany was prompt in purchasing them. When, a few years later, the celebrated Esterhazy diamonds came into the market, Tiffany & Co. paid over $100,000 for the portion selected by them. In 1887, when the crown jewels of France were offered, one-third of the list was purchased by the same firm, at a cost of about $500,000, being a larger amount than the total purchases of the nine next largest buyers. Many other sparkling memorials came from time to time, each contributing its share in the establishing of the reputation and business policy of the house.

In 1850, Mr. Gideon F. T. Reed, a leading jeweller of Boston, was admitted into the partnership. A branch house was established in Paris, and Mr. Reed became the resident partner in Paris, where the house was conducted under the firm name of Tiffany, Reed & Co. This enabled the firm to take advantage of any fluctuation of prices in the European markets, and proved to be an excellent business venture. The rapid growth of the Paris branch necessitated several changes of location, and since the retirement of the late Mr. Reed, the foreign branch has been conducted under the name of Tiffany & Co. Americans resident or travelling abroad have for years been large patrons of the Paris house.

The manufacture of sterling silverware was begun in 1881, and Mr. Tiffany could not be satisfied with anything short of the highest modern attainments. It was his ambition to rival in purity of materials and in fineness of workmanship the celebrated silversmiths of Europe. Only the most skilful artisans were employed. Mr. Tiffany discovered in the work of John C. Moore a strength and individuality wholly different from that of any other silversmith, and an arrangement was naturally agreed upon whereby Mr. Moore was to manufacture solely for Tiffany & Co. Upon his retirement, Edward C. Moore, his son, was chosen to fill his place. The skill the latter had acquired under his father's tuition, together with the resources of the firm, soon gave a wonderful impetus to the aspiring industry. The work-rooms gradually grew from the first small shop with a few workmen into the present huge block of brick and iron on Prince Street, a busy hive of artisans and artists to the number of 500. One of the first innovations was that of using the highest practical grade of silver. Old Spanish and Mexican coins had previously furnished a large part of the metal used, but these varied greatly in fineness. Tiffany & Co. introduced the English standard of sterling silver, $\frac{925}{1000}$ fine, the highest practical standard for articles in use.

In 1853, the firm was again reorganized by the retirement of Mr. Young and Mr. Ellis, and the addition of several junior partners, and the name was then changed to Tiffany & Co. In the following year larger and better accommodations were secured at 550 Broadway. In 1858, Mr. Tiffany again gave evidence of his quick perception of historic values in the purchase of the unused portion of the first Atlantic cable, including twenty miles or more. These he cut up into suitable lengths, made them into paper weights, canes, umbrella and whip handles, bracelets, watch charms, etc., mounted them in various styles, and sold them as souvenirs at profitable prices. So eager were the multitudes to secure these mementoes that policemen were employed to maintain order.

As a citizen, Mr. Tiffany prized his citizenship, and, although taking no active part in politics, he always showed himself to be a public-spirited American. In 1861, when the Civil War began, it became necessary for men to show where they stood. Many were irresolute and some were openly opposed to the Government. Mr. Tiffany's patriotism showed itself in no uncertain way. Hardly had the echoes of the first shot fired upon Sumter died away before the Tiffany store front, on Broadway, blazed with flags and the windows shimmered with steel. Mr. Tiffany personally submitted to Quartermaster-General Meigs a complete model of the equipments of the French Army, then supposed to be the best in Europe. Even the silverware and jewelry were displaced to make room for military accoutrements, and the agents of the house then in Europe were instructed to purchase the best weapons, army clothing, ambulances, army shoes and war materials and equipments that could be obtained. Orders began to pour in for swords for the use of officers, badges, medals and all metallic art work used in the grim play of war. His factories were enlarged and his forces increased, for the best were considered none too good for the loyal defenders of the Government who were to use them, and only "the best" could emanate from Tiffany's workshops. Mr. Tiffany became a most earnest supporter of the cause of the North, and gave liberally of his time and means.

During the draft riot in 1863, his establishment was threatened by the mob as it moved down Broadway, but the police intercepted and defeated the rioters above Bleecker Street, thus preventing the warm reception that Mr. Tiffany had prepared for them.

The war caused a large extension of the business of the house, and in 1868 the firm was incorporated as a manufacturing company, with a capital of $2,400,000. Mr. Tiffany was made its President and Treasurer, which offices he still holds. Mr. Charles T. Cook, who, upon the retirement of Mr. Reed, in 1875, was elected Vice-President and Assistant Treasurer, has been Mr. Tiffany's chief support during the past twenty-five years, and to his executive abilities and good judgment, Mr. Tiffany ascribes much of the success that has come to the house.

The incorporation of the house was attended with a general extension of the business. The manufacture of watches and clocks was added to their other manufactures. The silver works were enlarged, and Mr. Edward C. Moore, who had become a director in the company, was made manager of the manufacturing interest.

In 1868, a branch house was established in London, and this was followed by the construction of a large plant for the manufacture of watches at Geneva, the largest factory of its kind in Switzerland.

Thirty years of success in business were sufficient to change the direction of trade. The house which began by importing goods from Europe now became a large exporter of American silverware to Europe. One after another the crowned heads and royal personages of the Old World made Mr. Tiffany their "silversmith by appointment," while from France and Russia he received special distinctions. The gradually expanding business again called for increased room. About this time the Church of the Puritans, at the corner of Broadway and Fifteenth Street, was offered for sale, and was promptly purchased by Tiffany & Co. This gave them a frontage of 78 feet on Broadway and 140 feet on Fifteenth Street. A fine five-story fire-proof building was at once erected, and was opened for business November 10, 1870. This building afforded better opportunities for the display of goods than any they had previously occupied. It also gave them immense fire-proof and burglar-proof vaults and safes for the storage of the large stock of precious stones, watches, jewelry and other valuable goods. It is admirably suited in every respect to the conduct of the immense business done by this honorable and widely known house.

The latest addition to the business is the manufacture of electro silver-plated ware.

A seven-acre plot was secured at Forest Hill, a suburb of Newark, N. J., upon which a building, covering 45,000 square feet, has just been erected, to be devoted specially to this branch of the business.

The Tiffany exhibits at the several International Expositions have, in every case, been conspicuous and noteworthy, and have reflected great credit upon the achievements of the house, and honor upon American ingenuity and skill. At the Paris Exposition of 1867, they were honored with the first award for American silverware, this being the first instance in which such an honor was ever conferred upon a foreign exhibitor.

At the Centennial Exhibition, in 1876, Tiffany & Co.'s exhibit of their masterpieces in the various departments, left them practically without competitors. At the Universal Expositions, held at Paris, in 1878 and 1889, the house again received the *Grand Prix* for silverware, with a large number of other medals for the different departments of their exhibits. Mr. Tiffany, who personally attended the Exposition of 1878, was made a Chevalier of the National Legion of Honor of France, and from the Emperor of Russia he received the gold medal *Præmia Digno*—an exceptional tribute. Tiffany & Co. were appointed Imperial and Royal Jewellers, Gold and Silversmiths to most of the monarchs and dignitaries of Europe.

Perhaps no exhibit at the World's Columbian Exposition was more frequently referred to or more favorably commented upon than the exhibit of this house. The London *Art Journal* speaks of it as " a display more varied in expression and original in design, more distinctive and individual than the work of any other firm in the Art Metal Group. * * * One may well be in doubt whether our much-boasted European pre-eminence in these things is to last much longer, and whether, after all, we shall not, in the near future, be compelled to regard the firms of New York as at least our equals, if not our superiors, in the production of high-class gold and silver work."

Over fifty awards were granted to Tiffany & Co. for their varied exhibits at Chicago. The value of the articles displayed would require at least seven figures to express, and the cost of the pavilion with its arrangements exceeded $200,000.

Before the close of the war, and for some time after, the facilities of Tiffany & Co. were taxed to their utmost with orders for testimonials of every description for presentation to the heroes of the battles. Hundreds of richly mounted testimonial swords were made, many of them set with precious stones and costing from $500 to $10,000. Perhaps the most notable of these was the sword presented by Tiffany & Co. to the great Sanitary Fair, held in New York City, in 1864. The scabbard was of gold and richly studded with rubies, diamonds and sapphires, representing the national colors. The votes were sold at $1 each, and realized for the Fair nearly $100,000. General Grant received the highest number of votes and the sword. General McClellan was a close competitor.

Among the many other testimonial swords

made by Tiffany & Co. were the swords presented to General W. T. Sherman after the battle of Shiloh; to General Fremont, the pathfinder of the West; to Major-General Halleck, by the ladies of St. Louis; and to Major-General Burnside, by the State of Rhode Island.

Many of the finest medals and presentation pieces produced in this country have also been turned out by this house. Conspicuous among these are the gold medal presented by the Government to Cyrus W. Field upon the completion of the Atlantic Cable, in 1866; the gold medal to the arbitrators of the *Alabama* claims in 1873; the silver centrepiece, "Liberty Enlightening the World," to August Bartholdi, from 121,000 Americans, in 1886; the silver centrepiece to William E. Gladstone, by American admirers in recognition of his efforts to secure Home Rule for Ireland, 1887.

The Bryant Vase, presented to William Cullen Bryant by his friends in commemoration of his eightieth birthday, and which was on exhibition at the Centennial, was universally pronounced to be the most artistic and notable production of the time. A few of the most recent yachting and other trophies were shown in the loan collection of Tiffany & Co.'s exhibit at the Columbian Exposition.

As a representative business man, Mr. Tiffany has been honored with many positions of trust, and few philanthropic or other public movements have been inaugurated in the metropolis without his aid and support. He is a liberal patron of art, and in its advancement in this country he has shown the keenest interest.

Mr. Tiffany was one of the founders of the New York Society of Fine Arts, and of the Union League Club of New York. He is a Trustee of the Metropolitan Museum of Art, and of the American Museum of Natural History; a Fellow of the Geographical Society and of the National Academy of Design. He is a director in several banks, security and trust companies, and is numbered among the millionaires of the metropolis. He is a member of the New York

Historical Society; of the American Protective Tariff League; of the Chamber of Commerce; of the Young Men's Christian Association, and life-member of many charitable and philanthropic organizations.

While Mr. Tiffany's name is inseparably associated with every stage of development of the house, he has always been ready to recognize and commend the services of his associates and co-laborers, and he never speaks of his business career without feelingly referring to those whose earnest labors in the various branches of the business and departments of its manufactures have contributed so much to Tiffany & Co.'s success.

THE SKETCHES
CONSTITUTING THIS VOLUME
ARE TAKEN
FROM THE TWELVE NUMBERS OF "TRADE"
FOR 1893,
A MAGAZINE DEVOTED TO THE INTERESTS
OF THE MERCHANT, THE BUSINESS MAN,
THE CLERK, AND THE HOME.
THIS MAGAZINE IS PUBLISHED MONTHLY BY
THE GIRARD PUBLISHING COMPANY,
PHILADELPHIA, PA.
AND ITS READERS REGARD IT
THE BRIGHTEST, THE MOST HELPFUL, THE
BEST OF ALL THE TRADE JOURNALS
SUBSCRIPTION PRICE, ONE DOLLAR A YEAR.
SEND 10 CENTS FOR SAMPLE COPY.

www.ingramcontent.com/pod-product-compliance
Lightning Source LLC
Chambersburg PA
CBHW032226230426
43666CB00033B/1604